Confessions of a Mountie

Confessions of a Mountie

MY LIFE BEHIND THE RED SERGE

Frank Pitts

FLANKER PRESS LIMITED
ST. JOHN'S

Library and Archives Canada Cataloguing in Publication

Pitts, Frank, 1958-, author
   Confessions of a Mountie : my life behind the red serge / Frank Pitts.

Issued in print and electronic formats.
ISBN 978-1-77117-542-5 (paperback).--ISBN 978-1-77117-543-2 (html).--ISBN 978-1-77117-544-9 (html).--ISBN 978-1-77117-545-6 (pdf)

   1. Pitts, Frank, 1958-. 2. Royal Canadian Mounted Police--Biography. 3. Police--Newfoundland and Labrador--Biography. I. Title.

HV7911.P58A3 2016   363.2092   C2016-902506-3
                                   C2016-902507-1

© 2016 by Frank Pitts

ALL RIGHTS RESERVED. No part of the work covered by the copyright hereon may be reproduced or used in any form or by any means—graphic, electronic or mechanical—without the written permission of the publisher. Any request for photocopying, recording, taping, or information storage and retrieval systems of any part of this book shall be directed to Access Copyright, The Canadian Copyright Licensing Agency, 1 Yonge Street, Suite 800, Toronto, ON M5E 1E5. This applies to classroom use as well. For an Access Copyright licence, visit www.accesscopyright.ca or call toll-free to 1-800-893-5777.

PRINTED IN CANADA

This paper has been certified to meet the environmental and social standards of the Forest Stewardship Council® (FSC®) and comes from responsibly managed forests, and verified recycled sources.

Edited by Robin McGrath   Cover Design by Graham Blair   Cover photo by Scott Ross

FLANKER PRESS LTD.
PO BOX 2522, STATION C
ST. JOHN'S, NL
CANADA

TELEPHONE: (709) 739-4477   FAX: (709) 739-4420   TOLL-FREE: 1-866-739-4420
WWW.FLANKERPRESS.COM

9 8 7 6 5 4 3 2 1

   Canada Council   Conseil des Arts
                        for the Arts   du Canada

We acknowledge the [financial] support of the Government of Canada. *Nous reconnaissons l'appui [financier] du gouvernement du Canada*. We acknowledge the support of the Canada Council for the Arts, which last year invested $153 million to bring the arts to Canadians throughout the country. *Nous remercions le Conseil des arts du Canada de son soutien. L'an dernier, le Conseil a investi 153 millions de dollars pour mettre de l'art dans la vie des Canadiennes et des Canadiens de tout le pays.* We acknowledge the financial support of the Government of Newfoundland and Labrador, Department of Tourism, Culture and Recreation for our publishing activities.

This book is dedicated to the most important person in my life. She has been there in good times and bad, and always had a positive smile. She has been strong when I have been weak. She has been solid when I have been broken, and she has moved forward with strength when I have fallen down. She has found strength to forgive when I have wronged. Only a fortunate few have been lucky enough to bond so closely with another such that you act as one, my soulmate. Others who know her always introduce her as "the Mountie's wife." I call her Diane.

Contents

Prologue 1

1	Day Start	5
2	The Early Years	11
3	Who They Are	21
4	The Dark Side	29
5	First Lessons	47
6	The Purple Slipper	53
7	The Art of Training	65
8	A Baseball Bat	75
9	Seeing and Believing	79
10	Some Long Days	85
11	The Toothache	93
12	Little Red Cross	99
13	A Tragic Disappearance	107
14	So Easy to Die	113
15	Saving Christmas	121
16	A Questionable Decision	131

17	The Takedown	137
18	You Have Got to Be Kidding Me	143
19	The Process	149
20	Justice on Trial	153
21	A New Day	165

Epilogue 167

Acknowledgements 173

Confessions of a Mountie

While visiting Canada with his parents, this young boy from Johannesburg, South Africa, got lost. I found him crying on the roadside. Photo taken in June 1984.

— Prologue —

Cautiously and, yes, a little scared, I opened the car door and stepped outside. Behind the cover of the driver's door, I stood quietly, in full working RCMP patrol uniform, minus the hat. I was alone. The adrenalin rush on the way here had left me with a mild shiver and a burning in my gut. I was not feeling cold, but I felt a shiver nonetheless.

Then, suddenly, without warning, there was a crash as the basement door burst open, and a man came stampeding out. He had a huge machete raised high above his head. He charged at me, screaming with rage as if he were part of the soundtrack of a bloody horror show. Despite his roaring voice muffling the words somewhat, his message to me was very clear.

"Shoot me, you fucking pig, shoot me!"

With no memory of doing so, I had ripped my semi-automatic RCMP-issued pistol from its holster and locked it onto his centre mass. With no rehearsal, I yelled, "Police! Stop! Drop that damn knife!"

He froze. He was standing twenty feet away, and he began a series of screams. "Shoot me, asshole, shoot me! Go ahead, you fucking pig, shoot me! Come on, whattaya waitin' for? Shoot me, or I'll cut your guts out! Shoot me, you stupid pig, shoot me!"

I yelled back, "Put down the damn knife! Don't be stupid!"

This was surreal. I wondered, *Can this be happening? What the hell is going on?*

Just seconds before this, with no lights or siren, my police car had rounded the corner onto his street. There sat his house, an older two-storey with a ground-level entry. The gravel driveway which bordered the right side of the house was about forty feet long and ended at the right bottom side-entry door. I had hurriedly rolled into his driveway and had then radioed my arrival at the scene.

"Dispatch, Five Alpha One."

"Dispatch here. Go ahead, Five Alpha One."

"I am ten-twenty-three. You can mark me ten-seven scene."

"Ten-four. Copy that," replied Dispatch.

The ten-code is a list of numeric assignments given to concise phrases used in radio communication by law enforcement and other emergency responders. "Ten-twenty-three" indicates that police have arrived at the location of the complaint. "Ten-seven" relayed that the officer was now busy with a complaint and unavailable for any other calls for service. I was definitely unavailable to address anything else at that moment. I was unequivocally ten-seven scene.

I slammed the car's transmission into park. I could hear the gravel crunch under the weight of the sudden stop. I pocketed the keys.

My heart was pounding. It felt like it was coming out of my chest. He yelled again, "Come on. Shoot me!"

I yelled back with equal thrust, "Put down the damned knife! No one is getting hurt."

He screamed again, "You asshole pig, I'm going to cut you up!"

I pleaded again, "Settle down, okay? No one gets hurt."

My directions were met with more profanity, more pleading to shoot, more screaming outbursts. He wanted to die. He wanted to die right at that instant. I wondered where the hell my backup was. Three police units had responded to this complaint, and somehow I stood alone. I did not hear another vehicle. Where the hell did my backup go? My heart was now racing. I needed to settle down. Many questions flashed through my mind. Was he going to charge me? If he did, could I shoot him? Was he intent on killing me? Why was he doing this? How the hell did I get into this mess? How did this happen?

It had been a great day until now.

— Chapter 1 —
Day Start

Every single event that has ever happened to you in your life is preparing you for an event that has yet to occur.

The day had started out normally, if there is such a thing in police work. For me, it was a regular day shift, 8:00 a.m. to 4:00 p.m. After this shift there were three more night shifts, then, finally, a much-needed day off. There is no other job that provides the unknowns, surprises, and varieties presented in police work. An entire shift can be spent doing nothing but routine patrols and paperwork. Conversely, an officer may be called to a car crash, a variety of accidents, deaths, traffic complaints, barking dogs, domestic disputes, break-ins, thefts, assaults, murders, or missing people. The list is endless and ever changing. No two shifts are ever the same; the variety is vast. Then, just when it appears that you have seen and done it all, you're given a new assignment where the only appropriate thought is, *You have got to be kidding me.*

Unbelievably, I once attended a call where a person complained that the neighbor's chickens were chasing her cat! I even spent several hours of one shift rounding up and capturing loose pigs that had escaped from a trailer that had rolled over on a highway! I was wrestling my own kind—imagine that!

As a police officer, one is always awake much too early in anticipation of what the day will bring. To combat the lack of sleep, there is coffee, and then more coffee. This call involving the standoff occurred when I was preoccupied at a gas bar, tasked to resolve a conflict between two drivers. The driver of the rear vehicle claimed that the front vehicle had backed up to get closer to the pump and struck him. The driver of the front vehicle claimed he was parked and the rear vehicle nudged up to get closer to the gas pump and struck him. Each was blaming the other. I had never seen this before, no, not at all. I have found that in almost every event, there is "his side of the story" and "her side of the story," and that somewhere in the middle you will usually find the truth. Over the years I found it difficult to accept that so many people lie, cheat, steal, exaggerate their stories, and hurt and murder others.

This incident at the gas pump was relatively minor compared to many other complaints I had been tasked with over the years. I had been going through the paces when this call came from Dispatch: "Five Alpha One. Dispatch."

"Five Alpha One here. Go ahead."

"What's your ten-twenty?" Ten-twenty is Dispatch asking for my location. I replied, "Just finishing up this accident on route ten."

"Could you attend the office ASAP?"

"Ten-four. I will be there in about five minutes."

This was usually a very bad sign. A call to return to the office to address a complaint usually meant that it was of a serious nature, that is, too sensitive to broadcast over the radio. If it were broadcast, then everyone in scanner-land would show up to see what was going on. An audience is something a police officer does not need, especially during a standoff.

I quickly wrapped up the traffic complaint, wished both drivers a happy life, and departed the gas bar. I then proceeded to the office in a hurry. Moments later, I arrived at headquarters and was immediately greeted by two other officers, Adam and Calvin, in the back parking lot. They were just boarding their own police cars. They briefed me quickly—and as I reflect back now, maybe just a little too briefly.

They advised me that Dispatch had received a call from a distraught, intoxicated, suicidal male. The man had said that he had his girlfriend held up in his house and that he had beaten her so badly that she may die. He had told Dispatch that if anyone came to help her, he was going to kill her and himself. He had said that it didn't matter who showed up—ambulance, police, whoever—they would die.

The suspect was well-known to police. He had a history of mental illness and was diagnosed as bipolar. His name was Burt.

Dispatch had tried to keep him on the phone, but they said it sounded like he had torn the phone from the wall. We were all intent on going to this home and resolving this issue without harm coming to anyone. We all felt that our arrival would de-escalate this in minutes. Usually in situations like this, all police officers had to do was knock on his door, verify that everything was all right, and, if justified, there may be an arrest. Normally this would be wrapped up in minutes.

We were all experienced police officers, and I was not sure about Calvin and Adam, but I had attended many calls like this one before. They usually turned out to be nothing. A call of this nature occurred very rarely in this small, rural Newfoundland community. We discussed the address, and we were satisfied that we all knew where we were going. I took the lead.

In convoy fashion, we all headed to the location. It was a typical older subdivision, houses occupied by low to moderate-income families. We used no lights or sirens, so as not to aggravate the situation. I arrived at the street where I believed Burt was residing, turned right, drove twenty feet, and turned left, pulling into Burt's driveway. I assumed that my backup was behind me.

Burt broke through the basement door with such rage that I had no time to ponder where my backup was any longer. I immediately had to engage. I learned much later that Calvin and Adam, thinking I was on the wrong street, had driven past. Then they wasted more time pulling over and waiting some distance away, wondering where the hell I had gone. They had then parked and were waiting for me to rejoin them! I'm not sure how long they waited there before turning around to see where I had gone. It may not have been long, but it felt like an eternity. They had been calling me on the radio, but I was so engaged with this distraught individual that I could not disengage to respond to them.

It was just Burt and me, both frozen. We were locked onto each other for what seemed like a lifetime. Maybe five minutes, maybe ten, it didn't matter—time had stood still. As we stared at each other, I realized that I was no longer shaking. I was not nervous, my heart had stopped racing, and I was calm. His yelling was echoing throughout the small neighbourhood. Screams were coming from a wide-open mouth that was rimmed with white froth. The thick foam was built up in the corners of his mouth, something I had seen before. It is some sort of metabolic reaction that occurs when a person has consumed vast quantities of alcohol. This guy was wasted, yet steady on his feet. He looked eight feet tall, but that was my adrenalin screwing up my usually accurate observations. In reality, he was only six foot two. He looked like he was 400 pounds, but that estimate was also off—he was only 250 pounds at best, but still a huge man by any measure. He was topped with dark, greasy hair with a receding hairline. In describing his appearance, unkempt would be an understatement. His eyes were bloodshot and his pupils were narrow, in contrast to his wide face. He was wasted, yet he was very much aware of the curved, two-foot-long machete he was holding. Except for the shining edge running the length of the blade, it was coated with a light rust. He stood there, jamming it toward me and yelling once again, "You stupid coward. Just shoot me!"

I responded, "I won't do that. Drop the knife!"

He continued to howl. It was obvious he didn't know what

was going on. This was not good. Where was my backup? This idiot wanted to die, and somehow I had been chosen as his executioner. How did I get here? This was not at all like when we were kids, playing cops and robbers or cowboys and Indians. This was no fun at all.

There was nothing in the innocence and simplicity of my youth that could have prepared me for this.

— Chapter 2 —

The Early Years

Parents rarely let go of their children, so children let go of them. Children grow up and move away. The moments that used to define them—a mother's approval, a father's hug—are now covered by moments of their own accomplishments. It is not until they have children of their own that they gain an understanding of their parents.

My story is no different or more special than the hundreds of thousands of other Canadians growing up in the 1950s and 1960s in remote parts of Canada. Everyone has a story. Sometimes they tell that story, but, sadly, all too often they do not. I have chosen to tell my story. It is nothing amazing, different, or unique. It's just mine.

I grew up in a small community in beautiful Freshwater, Newfoundland. Freshwater is nestled on the west corner of tiny Bell Island, just north of St. John's, surrounded by the cold North Atlantic Ocean.

My mother had eleven children—a small family by some standards. A family down the street from where we had lived had twenty children. My mother's eleventh was born four months after my father suddenly and tragically passed away from a botched gallbladder operation. He was only thirty-five years old.

I was just six years old, and I recall that day as though it were yesterday. It was a warm day in May, and I had been playing hopscotch around the back of our house when my older sister appeared from around the corner and said, "Frankie, you have to come inside."

I was reluctant to leave my game and somewhat angry regarding her demand. Really, what could be so important as to interrupt this hopscotch match that I had been winning? She begged, and I relented.

I entered my home, and there were a lot of people sitting around the kitchen: my siblings, my mom, some uncles, aunts, family friends, and a priest. A lot of them were sobbing. My sister whispered to me, "Daddy has died."

I didn't get it, and I don't recall reacting in any other way than wanting to get back to my hopscotch game. My father had been sick a lot. I don't have many memories of time with him, and I certainly didn't realize just how sick he was. I returned to play with my friends.

The next few days were busy. There were a lot of people, a lot of food, flowers, and many tears. It was kind of exciting, actually, because of all the attention our family was getting. I was just too young to understand what had happened, until the day of the funeral.

Many of the events during the bereavement and funeral have escaped me over time, except one. It was at the gravesite for the burial. I was standing alongside my family and relatives, wearing a dark suit that covered a neatly pressed white shirt and a blue tie. A large hole had been dug at the community cemetery, and everyone was standing around this hole. Several wooden planks were strung from one side to the other across this hole, and a large, neatly polished coffin sat on the planks. My father was inside that box. Yes, it is called a coffin, but to me it was simply a box. I wasn't really sure he was gone. But then, after the priest had said many words, none of which I understood, things changed for me. Several men slipped ropes under the coffin and pulled the ropes tautly. As they did this, it raised the coffin slightly, allowing other men to remove the planks. I was not prepared for what happened next. The men then slackened the ropes and began lowering the coffin. I thought, *What the hell are they doing?*

Inch by inch, the coffin was lowered until it disappeared into the ground. It hit me. A lump swelled in my throat, and tears began to flow. They were putting my dad in the ground. He was gone. He was not coming back. The brutal horror that he was put in a hole in the ground struck me hard. Then, as if that was not bad enough, two men with shovels started throwing dirt on him. I was in disbelief. Dad was in that box at the bottom of that hole, and he was now being covered with dirt. There was no doubt anymore that he was gone. I cried for days. I was afraid, and for the first time in my life, I felt so alone.

Mother's strength must have been phenomenal to get

through this. She was a young woman, yet committed to raising her eleven children on her own. We didn't have very much, but that doesn't matter when you don't realize it. There was never a vehicle in our family, yet we got everywhere we needed to go. I think I was seven or eight years old before we got our very first TV, a small black-and-white. There were no colour TVs back then, or, if there were colour TVs, there were none for sale in our small corner of the world.

The old homestead, all of 750 square feet, on Bell Island, Newfoundland and Labrador. Home to Mother and her eleven children.

There was little variety in fresh fruits or vegetables, yet we were never hungry. We didn't wear designer blue jeans, but mostly hand-me-downs, and we were never cold. Most of my sisters' clothes were hand-sewn by my mom. There were no iPhones, iPods, computers, or video games, yet we were always entertained.

There is no doubt that we were poor, but that was normal. We didn't know any better. We climbed hills and trees, splashed in the cold North Atlantic, skipped rocks, built tree houses, and constructed "trucksies," more commonly known as go-carts.

Many Saturday mornings, my childhood friend Ronnie and I dragged his father's dory from its perch to the shoreline and rowed out into the frigid North Atlantic to jig codfish. No bait was required on the jigger hook. A jigger is just a lump of lead moulded into the shape of a fish with two hooks on one end. The motion of pulling this jigger up and down with a line eventually hooks a codfish. Ronnie and I would fill the bottom of the boat in a couple of hours. Afterwards, we went door to door selling the cod for pennies. With enough pennies, we would spend the afternoon in the local bar drinking root beer and playing pool. Yes, kids were allowed in the bar back then. How cool was that? We had all we needed.

I fought with my brothers, and I even broke a sister's nose. I had been watching Bruce Lee martial arts movies and was practising some self-created moves. I was showing my sister how close my fist could come to her face without touching her. However, I had not perfected my skills. I guess I should have practised more!

I won fights, but mostly I lost fights. I was a great search leader, one morning, when my older brother came running into the house yelling and crying, "I lost my bread, I lost my bread."

No problem, I thought, we didn't need to call the Mounties on this one. I could handle it. I gathered a posse of siblings to go find his bread. The search zone was near our chicken coop. We managed to decipher from my distraught brother that he had jumped from the chicken coop onto the ground, and in doing so, he lost his bread. No problem, we would find it. Oddly, though, the more we looked, the more upset he became. He was acting as though we were poking fun at him, which we were not. We were just intent on finding his bread.

What's his problem? I thought. We kept looking, until, finally, the mystery was solved. No, the bread was not found. Turns out my brother had jumped from the chicken coop and had lost his *breath*. That Newfoundland accent can definitely be misleading during a moment of childhood stress.

It was a simple life back then, but not all carefree. Mother needed all the help she could get. Unfortunately, some help was not appreciated. My mother had an old tub washing machine. I believe it was called a wringer washer. Inside the drum was a finned device that spun back and forth in rotation. I think that drum may have been called an agitator. This agitator literally beat the dirt out of clothing. Well, one of my siblings came up with the bright idea that we could help out our mother by washing the endless string of dishes using this machine. After all, everyone hated doing them by hand. While mother was outside one day, the dishes were thrown in, and that beast of a machine was fired up. That was a bad idea.

A few days later, I thought I could make it up to my mother for the wrong we had done. I decided to paint the clothesline for her. The line was old and faded, and I thought a fresh coat of white paint would restore it to its original shine. I did not realize that the old oil-based paint used back then took days to dry in the cold, damp Atlantic spring air. White stripes on clothing are a lot more common today than they were back then!

If it wasn't already hard enough for my mother, I had to shame her by committing a criminal act. I was ten years old. One of my friends had acquired a hula hoop, a thin plastic circular tube that you would swing around your waist, arms, or legs. Some people could even swing it with their neck. I decided that I had to have it. When the opportunity presented itself, I stole the hoop and hid it. I was not a very good criminal. Within hours, one of my siblings found it, and it was not long before the family investigation proved that I had stolen it. I didn't know what I was thinking, as it was well-known that my mother didn't have money to be throwing around for trivial things like hula hoops. How could I ever explain its acquisition? Regardless, I had been caught. Now for the punishment. I didn't know if I was going to be spanked, or if a curfew would be inflicted on me. I wasn't aware of any other kind of punishment. It had to be one of the two.

When the time was right, my mother called me to her room. I knew that some of my other siblings would be in the room next door with their ears pinned to the wall to hear my fate. I knew this because I had performed this type of eavesdropping myself.

I walked into the room, my head held low. I was expecting a strapping. My mother asked, "Why did you steal that thing?"

I replied, "I don't know why. I know that it was very stupid."

Then she startled me with words that promised a punishment I had not even contemplated. "What is your grandfather going to think when I tell him that the Mounties have taken you to jail?"

I was shocked! I didn't know what to say or do. There was no spanking, no curfew. This was way more severe a punishment than any others that Mother could have given me. I never thought that stealing could net you a jail sentence. For days after that, every knock on the door, every vehicle sound, was surely the Mounties coming to get me. But they never came. What's more important is that I never forgot. I didn't really know what jail was, but it was then and there that I decided it was a place that I would never be going. I never stole again.

Life for me as a child was carefree and grand, but like everyone else, I realized that this all changes when one grows up (that is, of course, for those of us who get that chance). I had many dreams as a child as to what I wanted to do when I left high school. Most of those dreams were centred around space travel and scientific things—in fact, my high school classmates had nicknamed me Professor. Being a police officer was not on that list.

I just had to settle him down. I felt I could handle this. Things would be all right as long as he didn't come any closer. If he did, I would have to shoot him, and I was confident that it would be justified. I was in a standoff. We were each locked onto each other. He wanted me to kill him, or he may have tried to kill me. This was a desire, a want, a begging I recognized. It was called suicide by cop.

I recalled from my training that there were two categories of suicide by cop. The first is when people have committed a crime and are being pursued by the police and decide that they would rather die than be arrested. These people may not otherwise be suicidal but may decide that life is not worth living if they are incarcerated. The second involves people who are already contemplating suicide, and who, for whatever reason, decide that provoking law enforcement into killing them is the best way to act on their desires. These individuals will provoke law enforcement into killing them by committing an act that leaves the law enforcement person with no alternative action. In situations like this, all too often, police are forced to shoot. This was what Burt wanted. He may have been surprised that I had not shot him yet. In all of my twenty years of service, I had not encountered this suicide-by-cop thing before.

It was a confrontation. A man wanted to die. Contrarily, I did not want to die. But I was very much aware that I might die if I made the wrong move. I had to make a decision. Sometimes, being a cop is not a whole lot of fun.

Cops. Who are they, anyway?

Chapter 3

Who They Are

During one of many lectures, my trainer explained that throughout a police officer's career he or she will be called "pig" many times. The trainer explained that it should not be a cause for you to lose your composure. He said to embrace it, as it stands for Pride, Intelligence, and Guts.

Many people don't know exactly who the police are. The only encounters the vast majority of people ever have with police officers are during traffic stops as a result of enforcement of our country's highway traffic laws, the most common being speeding violations. The officer approaches the vehicle and the driver's stomach begins to churn, followed by fumbling of wallets and glove compartment contents. I have seen it hundreds of times. People do not even know who the police person is, and yet they are afraid. Why is this? Why are people afraid? After all, police officers are just ordinary, everyday, normal people.

He is the person in the grocery lineup just ahead of you, and she is in the same lineup, just behind you. They both go home complaining about the price of milk and cheese, just like you. He is the assistant coach of your child's hockey team, and she is the mother of the child wearing number seven, on that same team.

She is the one sitting beside you, sick and coughing, waiting her turn at the doctor's office. He is the one who just left with a new prescription to battle his ulcer.

They come from all parts of this vast country and beyond. They grow up in the overcrowded streets of massive cities like Vancouver, Toronto, and Montreal, and they grow up in small prairie towns, like Yellow Grass, Saskatchewan, and places with names I cannot even pronounce. They come from the east, the west, and the isolated north. In order to be a member of the Royal Canadian Mounted Police, the first step is to be a Canadian. The fact is, members can originate from any corner of the planet, acquire Canadian citizenship, and as long as a person meets the other engagement prerequisites, they are in. I have known some to originate from the United Kingdom, from Iraq, Australia, and Pakistan. Mounties are from practically every corner of the planet.

Their parents are varied. Some are police officers, and sadly some are thieves. Parents consist of plumbers, doctors, perverts, priests, liars, and yes, lawyers, too. Most of them are really awesome people, and yes, some have issues. For some of them, there are no parents, and some have no families. They are rich and they are poor and everything in between. Their backgrounds are as varied and as different as the seasons. When they first join, most have no idea what police work is all about. Some join because they've watched too many glorified American cop shows when they were growing up and now have a distorted expectation. Some joined because Mommy and Daddy told them to join. Unfortunately, not all parents are knowledgeable as to the many stressful scenarios that police officers encounter in the course of their daily routines.

They are just people, nothing more, nothing less. What they do is just a job.

So, what is with the bad attitudes, the negative stigma, and the name-calling?

The most likely explanation for the origin of the slang "cop" is that it came from the old English verb "to cop," meaning to seize, capture, or snatch. This origin dates back almost two centuries. Before that time, the word may have evolved from the Latin word *capere*, meaning to seize or take. "Cop" also has other meanings, like "to cop out," meaning to withdraw or escape. There is also "cop a plea," meaning to admit to a lesser crime in return for a lesser punishment.

As with many words, there are several stories floating around suggesting various origins. The notion that "cop" is an acronym for "constable on patrol" is nonsense. Similarly, the word did not arise because earlier police uniforms had copper buttons or badges.

Police officers have many different nicknames, the more common one being "pigs." Where does this originate? If one were to research, there are literally dozens of origin explanations. Of those I have read, the most logical and apparently widely accepted goes right back to the year 1809.

Back in 1809, Sir Robert Peel of London, England, developed a passion for sandy-back pigs found in Ireland and began to breed them in Tamworth, England. Soon these pigs were known as Tamworth pigs. Pig slang was commonplace in Tamworth because of this. It was in 1829 that the relationship to police officers originated.

Politicians were concerned about the way London was policed, and Sir Robert Peel changed things. His changes resulted in the formation of the metropolitan police, and this is why police are referred to as "bobbies." They were Bobby's boys. Due to the association with Tamworth pigs, the police suffered the same fate as other Tamworth products. They became synonymous with pigs.

"Pig" was an expression used as early as the mid-1500s to refer to a person who was heartily disliked. It is still used today in that context. I'm sure everyone has heard someone speak of some moron's behaviour and say the words, "Oh, he is such a pig."

The origin of the nickname "fuzz" appears to be a mystery, and a police slang that never really caught on. It has been suggested that it came from the word "fussy," with the analogy that policeman were articulate and fussy, leading to the evolution of the nickname.

They are also often referred to as the men in blue. I am not sure where this came from, as blue is probably the least common colour of all the uniforms police officers wear. The "blue" most likely originated from American cop shows.

In the 1980s, the RCMP patrol cars were blue with white doors, until some financially conservative senior member discovered that white vehicles were a lot less expensive than coloured vehicles. In an effort to save money, the RCMP changed over to all-white cars, with rainbow-coloured stripes running the length of the vehicles' bodies. (I always wondered if they ever considered the cost of the high-gloss vinyl multicoloured stripe!) With this new colour scheme, truckers began calling the RCMP "the rainbow warriors," but this title was short-lived.

It doesn't matter what you call them—pigs, cops, or fuzz—they are all just people.

There is a stigma attached to being a Mountie that baffles me every time I see or hear it. It happens all too often. Let me explain.

A Canadian kid becomes a Mountie. Two weeks into his first posting, he decides that the night shifts and the brutal nature of the calls are not for him, so he quits. He moves on and pursues a successful thirty-year career in the insurance business. His entire adult life had nothing to do with police work. He is so far removed that the RCMP organization is foreign to him. He knows nothing about it. Yes, a long time ago he had tried to be a Mountie, but failed.

Then one evening, thirty or so years after he had left the RCMP, he drinks too much at a local bar. He decides to drive home and gets caught for impaired driving. Tomorrow's news headlines will no doubt read "Former Mountie Charged With Impaired Driving."

I could never get that one!

Many people think that in the morning, cops pour cornflakes into a bowl, sprinkle in some bullets, and add milk before washing it all down with coffee. The truth is, most of them sprinkle sugar and add milk, just like everybody else. How did they get there? Why did they join? Their reasons for joining are just as varied as the places they come from. Mine were no exception.

Following my youth, I had no clue on what I should do for a career, and on a whim I thought I would try forestry. I attended college for two years and acquired a certificate of technology in forest resources. I then pursued a brief career with Environment Canada, but my life took a drastic turn in the late summer of 1979.

At that time I had been working in the town of Gander, in central Newfoundland. One day, during a lunch break at a restaurant in that town, I was seated and awaiting my meal when a customer walked in. I recognized this customer as a college friend from a couple of years back. But he wasn't like everyone else. He was very muscular, with a military-style haircut, and he was well-dressed. He was certainly out of place in this area, where everyone else was dressed a little more casually and not quite in the same physical condition as him. Upon entering the restaurant, he nonchalantly scanned the area and spotted me. He then approached, and we chatted for a while. I was incredibly impressed with his demeanour, professionalism, and attitude.

He explained that he had just graduated from "Depot," a place I had not heard of before, located in Regina, Saskatchewan. He explained that this place was where Mounties trained. He told me many stories about that place. I was intrigued. In fact, his stories of this Depot impressed me so much that I had an immediate urge to go there.

The challenge of this training excited me. I didn't know what Mounties did, or who they were. I really didn't know what police officers did, either, or if it was the same thing. The only real knowledge I had about Mounties was that, when we were bad children, Mother or other adults would say, "You better be good, or the Mounties will put you in jail." As children growing up in rural Newfoundland, we only ever saw them if someone died, or fell over a cliff. It didn't matter. I was going to be a Mountie, and that was that. It was a spur-of-the-moment decision, with no research, no thought, and no planning. Absolutely! The decision was made. I was going to this place called Depot, and there was nothing that could stop me.

If I could go back and change things, pursue another career, would I? Not on your life. So, yes, cops, pigs, and fuzz are all normal people, just like other people, but they can and do change. The reasons are many, and change is inevitable. Once a police officer has had several years of exposure to the challenges of policing, many appear on the surface to become cold, abrasive, and lacking in the empathy they once had. But underneath that hard-cop attitude remains the innocence of who they once were.

— Chapter 4 —

The Dark Side

No one is above the law. Not a politician, a priest, a lawyer, a criminal, or a police officer. We are all accountable for our actions.

How is it that all these normal people who become police officers change? At their core, they are the same, but on the surface they have changed. They have been shaped and moulded into something else. Why is this?

It starts in training. RCMP training takes place in a multi-faceted facility called Depot. Depot is located at the city of Regina, in the province of Saskatchewan. In the RCMP's early days, Depot had a full horse stable and employed veterinarians. All trainees at the time learned the skill of horsemanship, hence the title "Mounties." In 1966, the RCMP abandoned this component of training. The horses were moved to a new facility outside of Ottawa, Ontario, where they participate in the world-famous RCMP musical ride.

All RCMP members train at Depot. There were exceptions in the past, when members were trained at other facilities. As an example, in the early 1970s, due to extensive hiring, Depot could not handle the overwhelming number of candidates. As a result, a number of members completed part of their training at Canadian Forces Base Penhold in Alberta.

In 1974, the RCMP began training women at Depot, with the first troop graduating in 1975. During training in 1981, a "troop" consisted of thirty-two persons, all male or all female. There were no mixed-gender troops at the time. There was extensive hiring during this era, and Depot was processing over thirty troops a year. Of this number, the vast majority were male, at a ratio of approximately one female troop for every ten male troops. The number of troops processed annually is basic economics of supply and demand. Some years have seen as few as two or three troops graduate from Depot.

Of the thirty-two candidates that make up a troop, not all will graduate. The troop to which I was assigned in 1981 lost a candidate in the first week, a nineteen-year-old lad from Quebec who was homesick for his family. We lost our second member two weeks later, a thirty-two-year-old missing his wife and family. However, we did keep the remaining thirty to the end, which is rare, as some troops dwindle to as low as twenty before graduation day.

This fantastic place called Depot was not at all what I had expected. I was not prepared for this place. I was expecting the skylarking that my college friend had described. He painted a false picture for me. His was a picture of all fun and games, but in reality, it was not so.

In April 1981, shortly after arriving there, I learned very quickly that Depot was a paramilitary institute. This means that the training and curriculum paralleled a military-style institute. "Yes, Corporal!" and "No, Corporal!" quickly became common phrases. Boots spit-shined and polished, bedsheets pressed, floors waxed, clothes hung in order—the regimental requirements were never-ending.

Training was hard. Very hard. A contingent of thirty-two men slept side by side in a huge dormitory. The room was long and narrow, with sixteen beds on one side, sixteen on the other. The configuration of beds on each side was two beds side by side with no separation, then a stall that was shared with your "pit" partner, then two more beds and a stall, and on and on. There was no privacy.

You were told when to go to bed, when to get up, when to eat, and being late for any scheduled detail was not an option. Your days started at six in the morning. Lights-out was at ten at night. Days were full, and evenings even fuller with extra required activities. These extra activities were geared to improve your weaknesses. For example, if you were a poor driver, then extra driving practice was required, or if you were a poor swimmer, extra time in the pool was a necessity.

The swimming component of training was the commencement of a Depot nightmare for me. No, growing up on an island in the North Atlantic surrounded by water does not mean you could swim. Earlier in this narrative, I said we "splashed in the cold Atlantic." I did not say I could swim, because, no, I could not swim. At Depot, that presented a problem. During that era while at Depot training, being a competent swimmer was one of the prerequisites in the successful completion of training. I wasn't sure why this was required. Was the thinking at the time that, as a Mountie, while on patrol, an officer may drive by a lake or ocean where someone was drowning, and there was this expectation that the officer jump out of the police car and swim out to the victim and perform a miracle lifesaving manoeuvre? Whatever the thinking, swimming was in the curriculum, and it required a passing grade. I had dreaded my first swimming class from day one.

Two weeks into training, I attended that first swimming class. I did not sleep well the night before. As a troop, we all showed up at the pool at the specified time, stripped off our uniforms, showered, and slipped on slim blue speedos. We entered the pool area.

The trainer immediately started yelling at us to form a single line along the pool edge. He then explained that each recruit would jump into the pool and swim to the other side and exit the pool. Based on swimming ability, recruits would be split into two groups: advanced and beginners. There was no category for non-swimmers. It was assumed that if you made it to Depot, that you were a swimmer was a given. Unfortunately for me, this was not so. Out of fear, I stood at the end of the line.

I was determined to succeed, so I watched the front of the line as, one by one, my troop mates jumped in. They jumped into the water, some feet first, others head first, and, using their arms and legs to propel themselves, they crossed to the other side and climbed out. It looked very easy. I could do this, I thought.

After I had observed a dozen or so of the others complete this swim test, my confidence grew. I left the end position on the line and moved up a few spots. After all, I did not want to be a loser. As I watched, every troop mate performed this task with ease. Then, finally, it was my turn. My heart was pounding. I thought I could do this. I stood on the pool edge, looked at the water, and realized I was about to do something I had never done before. I closed my eyes, held my breath, and jumped in. I could feel the cold water as it splashed around me. I figured there wouldn't be a problem if I touched the bottom with my feet and pretended to swim and bluffed my way across . . .

Shit.

I gasped, realizing that my feet weren't touching the bottom. Nothing ventured, nothing gained, so I kept holding my breath and started swinging my arms like a madman to reach the other side. I was kicking my legs like a horse trying to ward off a pack of wolves, all to no avail. After several seconds, I thought I must now be at the other side, so I opened my eyes to reach the pool wall and climb out.

I saw nothing but water. Panic set in as I realized I was going to drown. Then I felt something slip over my head and onto my shoulder. I grabbed it and viciously hung on for my life. I was then being pulled. I had grabbed a blue ring attached to a long pole. At the end of the pole, the trainer was grasping and pulling, now holding my head above the water.

The trainer yelled, "What's your name?"

Out of breath, coughing and gasping for air, I yelled back, "Pitts, sir!"

He yelled, "Pitts! No kidding, that fits perfect. Where are you from, Pitts?"

"Newfoundland, sir."

He yelled even louder, "Don't call me 'sir,' I work for a living!" He added, with an air of arrogance, "The Pitts from Newfoundland. Now that's a double strike. Get the hell out of my pool."

At that moment, I thought my dream of becoming a Mountie was done. There was no way I could get past this swimming issue. I struggled with it, lost sleep over it, and had pretty much accepted my failure. But I was young and had something to prove, so I dug in. I embraced the challenge and spent countless hours in the pool to overcome this weakness. The first few swims bobbing around the pool with a little flotation pillow were embarrassing, to say the least, but I hung on, and eventually ditched the pillow and began to swim. Six months and 300 gallons of swallowed pool water later, after countless hours of extra time in the water, I had completed the mission. I was now a swimmer. This was my greatest Depot accomplishment. And it had nothing to do with police work!

To determine where a graduating recruit would be posted, staffing put a big map of Canada on the wall, tagged the recruit's name to a dart, and fired the dart at the map! Wherever the dart hit was the new assigned posting for the recruit. I'm not sure what happened to you if the dart failed to stick and fell to the floor.

As a result of the staffing team's method of recruit posting following graduation from Depot, some officers did not adjust well to their new posting and left the RCMP to join other municipal and provincial police services. This decision was usually made so the recruit could be closer to family and home. Our troop in 1981 lost two more police officers this way.

In addition to training new RCMP members, Depot had also been a major continuing education centre, delivering updated and highly specialized training to experienced RCMP officers and to members of other forces from all over Canada and around the world.

No one can be a regular member of the RCMP without completing the academy's twenty-four-week cadet training program. The exception was when police officers who had been trained at other police training facilities joined the RCMP. However, they first had to complete a modified and condensed RCMP training session at Depot.

The training facility at Depot was very progressive and always changing. It altered its curriculum to adjust to the social and economic changes of Canadian society. As needed, it would focus more on knowledge relating to the multiple facets of law enforcement than on military discipline. In the 1960s, 1970s, and 1980s, the RCMP training had a six-month, thorough, military-based component. In more modern times, the faces of cadets have changed. They are now on average ten years older than in past years and, decade after decade, the ratio of college- and university-educated applicants have kept increasing. This higher maturity level of trainees required fewer disciplinary actions and enabled the instructors to focus on the very demanding requirements of modern police work.

Although the training is very good and sometimes labelled as excellent, it cannot prepare a normal human being for everything encountered in the real world of police work. Training happens behind secure walls and fences. The general public may think that no issue is too much for a police person because they believe "they train for that." Well, in truth, they do not.

In training, mistakes are made and laughed about and can be corrected. In real life, mistakes can kill. At Depot, actors are used in confrontational training scenarios and know when to stop. In the real world, criminals do not. During police driving training, the vehicle can be pushed beyond its limits, and if the driver misses a corner, he or she will go for a hilarious slide across an open field. In real life, if a person crashes, all too often people die. Training does not prepare an officer to see that when a snowplow crashes into oncoming traffic, it shreds more than just the vehicle.

Imagine a job where every time you answer the phone, someone on the other end is complaining about something. No matter how trivial, or how serious, they expect you to provide an instant solution. Sometimes that instant solution is possible, but often it is not. The result is that an officer is often berated and cursed. One morning in my first year of service, I received a call that reported a SIDS, or sudden infant death syndrome. I rushed to the victim's residence at four in the morning to find a young father collapsed in tears on the doorstep. Inside, a young mother was holding her baby boy, whose body was now cold. He was seven months old. What training enabled me to humanely remove his limp body from her locked arms? I had to take from her the most precious gift she had ever known. How could I do this? There's no training for this reality.

I recall handling my first case of suicide by shotgun in the mouth. In training, they didn't explain that due to the elasticity of human tissue, when the blast first occurs there is a millisecond or two where the head blows up to two or three times its normal size before finally bursting from the pressure, exploding its contents. Nor were you told that you would see this image over and over thirty-five years later. It didn't prepare you for the next twenty-five or so suicides, nor the dozen or so murders.

A single old man slid into bed at his home and, overnight, quietly passed away from an apparent heart attack. He had no family. A neighbour finally called police after noticing that postal mail and junk flyers were accumulating on his front porch. Upon receiving the call, I attended. There was nothing in training to prepare me for what came next. This old man had died in September, and based on the last mail he had retrieved, and the page to which his TV guide was open, it was evident that he had been lying there for three months. It was now November. He had been lying and fermenting in his heated home for this entire period. No words can describe the stench emanating throughout the home. Training failed me on that one. As if that wasn't bad enough, the coroner arrived and needed assistance placing the body in a body bag. We rolled the victim off the bed, revealing a sea of millions of maggots. I guess I slept through that chapter in training.

In taking a statement from a sobbing eleven-year-old girl about how she was sexually violated by her uncle, training cannot prepare an officer to stay professional, swallow the lump in his throat, and hold back the tears of empathy he feels for this little girl.

Of the hundreds of traffic tickets I issued over the years to offending drivers, never once did a driver say, "Thank you, sir, I really deserved this. Keep up the good work!" The more common respond was, "Why aren't you out catching real criminals?" Or another favourite response: "What, got nothing better to do, you pig?"

I would usually ask the driver, "Do you know how fast you were going?" and all too often the reply was, "I have no idea." My response to this was, "You don't know how fast you were going? I guess I can write anything on the ticket that I want, huh?"

Once in a while, the driver would accuse me of trying to make my monthly ticket quota. I was always anxious to answer that one: "No, sir, they don't give us quotas anymore. They used to, but now we can write as many tickets as we want!"

Three or four years in, and you figure you have seen and done it all. Not so. Darren was my shift partner. We had worked side by side for three years. We worked well together. He knew my next move, and I knew his. We became close friends, both on and off shift. Darren had eight years' service and was well on his way to a great career. His first eight years were impeccable. He had been dating the same girl for over two years, and at Christmastime he offered her an engagement ring and a marriage proposal, which she accepted. They were to be married the following summer. Then, a week later, in the early morning hours of New Year's Day, a horrific event occurred at Darren's home that to this day has never made sense to anyone who knew him.

Darren unlocked and removed his RCMP-issued revolver from its security case. He loaded the revolver with six rounds of ammunition. He lay prone on his bed, with his head resting on his pillow. He placed the barrel of the revolver into his mouth. Darren squeezed the trigger . . .

The last time I had cried that hard was when my father's box was lowered into the ground. Darren's suicide was not only senseless, but no one could even suggest a viable theory as to why he had done this. The day of the funeral was particularly hard. For the first time in my service, I witnessed a sea of red serge like I had not seen before. Members came from near and far to pay their respects.

Only a week before Darren died, we had been working a night shift. Late in the night, while doing up some paperwork, I left my police notebook on my desk. When the opportunity presented itself, Darren stuck a little rainbow sticker on the face of the book. Underneath the rainbow were printed the words "You're special." At the time, I was very angry with Darren for doing this. I remember saying to him, "How bloody professional is it going to look when I have to use this notebook in court and everyone sees the damn rainbow on there?" I wish now that I had not said that. I left the sticker on there.

Then the most difficult thing I had ever had to watch in my life was repeated. Darren's brilliantly crafted coffin sat above a hole in the ground. It was not supported by wooden planks, as technology had evolved. It sat on top of a mechanical four-cornered stainless steel winch device. Two nylon straps were attached to two rollers and stretched across the hole to support the coffin. Cranking the device would spin some gearing that gently dropped the nylon straps, which in turn lowered the coffin into the ground. It didn't matter that it wasn't men with ropes. It was just as hard. That lump was in my throat again, almost choking me as, inch by inch, the coffin disappeared into the ground. I do not like funerals.

We never solved the mystery as to why Darren had taken his own life, but the fact that he had planned it for some time eventually became clear. Back then, most police officers had rechargeable flashlights. The batteries in these flashlights last for years; it was not a flashlight that you would open very often. One of Darren's co-workers, our friend Mark, had one of these flashlights. About ten months after Darren passed away, Mark's battery wouldn't take a charge anymore so he opened the device to replace it. The battery slipped out, and there was a sheet of white paper wrapped around it. Mark unwrapped the paper and experienced a chill as he read a note that had been written by Darren: "I'm sorry I did this to you guys. I will miss you all. Love, Darren."

When you walk into a police office today, you are greeted by security cameras and bulletproof glass. You do not talk to a human being face to face, but instead you talk through a small hole in the glass or you speak into a microphone. It wasn't always like that. There was a time when you walked into a police office and found yourself in an open and unsecured foyer furnished with a waist-high countertop. No cameras, and no glass. You would find yourself face to face within arm's reach of an office receptionist, or a police officer. That all changed in September 1980 when an armed suspect walked into the Richmond, British Columbia, RCMP detachment and opened fire in the open concept office. One police officer was shot in the chest and died instantly. A second police officer was shot in the thigh and survived. The suspect surrendered shortly afterwards outside the detachment.

It was at that time that RCMP management realized that the police and office staff were sitting ducks in the insecure offices. So, slowly, from west to east, office by office, secure barricades were constructed, the same impersonal barriers that you are greeted by today.

The first office that I had worked at in 1981 did not yet have its new barricade. It was still open concept. As with many other police officers, I didn't think it was a big deal. Few of us thought we were vulnerable, and as a result, few precautions were taken within the office environment. I would never have guessed that my first armed standoff would happen in this environment, but I was so young, green, immature, and naive about what humans were capable of that, at the time it occurred, I didn't even realize it was a standoff!

It was in November of 1981, and I had all of two months' service. Except for training scenarios, I had no experience relevant to confrontations involving armed suspects. The civilian office staff completed their shift at 4:00 p.m., and my trainer's shift finished at 5:00 p.m., leaving me alone on shift until 6:00 p.m. One whole hour alone. What could possibly go wrong?

I was spending that hour sitting in the front office, doing up some paperwork, when at approximately 5:45 p.m., the front door smashed open and a crazed man burst in, yelling and screaming. He was wielding a long axe in both hands, and when he spotted me he began screaming at me, telling me what an asshole I was, and many other names that I don't care to print. He was very dirty-looking, and for the first time I saw a white foam ring around a person's mouth, and built up in the corners, indicative of someone who was completely intoxicated.

As I look back now, I know that I would have been justified in drawing my revolver and opening fire and killing this man, but I didn't. As a matter of fact, I didn't even draw my revolver. I'm not sure if I was shocked or oblivious to the threat, but I took no evasive action. I did wonder, however, why this person, whom I didn't even know, held such a grudge toward me. As he yelled and screamed, it just seemed surreal, almost like an act. I remember feeling safe: there was a counter in front of him, and a desk in front of me, and he couldn't possibly reach me through those two obstacles.

As he screamed and pounded the axe on the counter, I heard a familiar dialect. He sounded like a Newfoundlander. I didn't yell back at him, I didn't beg him to drop the axe, and I didn't plea for him to settle down. Either I was unaware of the potential threat, or just stupid—I'm not sure exactly which—but instead of escalating the situation with verbal commands and a weapon pointed at him, I said, "You sound like a Newfoundlander. Are you from Newfoundland?"

With that, he kind of went blank, looked at me strangely, and with slurred speech said, "How did you know that?"

I replied, "'Cause I'm from Newfoundland. I recognize your accent."

With this, the suspect now seemed completely messed up, and he settled down. He was obviously torn between the fact that he was now in the presence of a fellow Newfoundlander, and the fact that this Newfoundlander was wearing a uniform. He then asked, "Well, where you from?"

"Bell Island," I replied.

With a slight laugh, he responded, "Go on, b'y!"

Then, as luck would have it, Constable Jones, who was scheduled in at 6:00 p.m., arrived early, entering through the rear staffing office door. He heard the commotion and quietly approached the suspect from the opposite side of the entrance. When Constable Jones was close enough, he lunged onto the suspect's back, swung his arm around the suspect, and locked his neck between his bicep and forearm, squeezing tightly. This rendered the suspect unconscious, a textbook carotid control application. Oddly enough, I remember thinking at the time, *Was that really necessary?*

This suspect had been upset with the actions taken toward him by another police officer over some logging conflicts, and for the first time I realized a new stigma that comes with wearing a uniform. We are all tarred with the same brush. If Constable A screws up, everyone out there sees that Constables B, C, D, and E also screwed up. There is no differentiation between officers. There is only one uniform, and we are all the same.

I have seen enough death to last ten lifetimes, as have most police officers. One by one, they pick away at your soul. Slowly, it jades you. The constant onslaught of incidents where people are in crisis changes your attitude about society. All the hurt you see, the fighting, the stealing, the deceptions, the greed, the cheating, and the abuse of children, can make a person cynical, cold, and abrasive.

A policeman is on his day off, going for a relaxing Sunday drive with his wife through a neighbourhood. They spot an eleven-year-old boy riding what appears to be a new bicycle. The wife says, "Looks like our neighbour, Nathan, has a new bike." The police officer will reply, "Yeah, he probably stole it." From what he has seen and done on the job, there is no more appropriate response.

Yes, police officers, who are still people, will change. How could they not? Hence the stigma, the name-calling, the attitudes, and the ugliness. Just when they get used to all the new experiences and believe that they have seen and heard it all, they will find that there are still more lessons to be learned. Surviving a standoff teaches but one. There have been and will be others.

His oversized plaid shirt had three bottom buttons holding it closed. It was flapping gently, stirred by the steady northeast wind that was blowing directly across the lawn. The wind was cold, very cold. His oversized, baggy blue sweatpants did little to warm him. They did, however, hide the bulges of fat resulting from years of ugly eating.

This was going nowhere, I thought. He was not dropping the machete.

I yelled again. "You're being stupid. Put down the damned knife. We can work this out."

His response was the same. "Shoot me! Shoot me! Shoot me! You're a chickenshit coward. You stupid-ass cop!"

I was there alone. There was no backup. I had never been attacked like this before. I looked back over the years at all the lessons I had learned. None of those lessons had prepared me for this.

At least, that was how I felt at the time.

— Chapter 5 —

First Lessons

Experience is something that you get shortly after you need it.

My thoughts often drift back to the beginning of my career and all I had seen and done over the years to get here. It has been an unforgettable journey, to say the least.

The six months Mounties spend at Depot do not conclude their training. It is the first of many steps. When new recruits arrive at their first posting, they are each assigned to an experienced police officer who will guide them through the myriad of challenges they will encounter over the next six months, or longer, if needed. This officer will train a new recruit to be effective as a police officer in the real world. His or her experience will provide the recruit with the necessary skill set to adapt and survive in the profession. I was once told that the greatest police officer is that person who has the ability to absorb the best character traits from numerous other police officers and mould them all into one skill set. That's easier said than done.

I recall an event on my very first journey to my new posting to the west coast of British Columbia. After disembarking from my flight and acquiring a rental vehicle, I was on my way. I stopped at an automated teller machine to get some cash. I was the cock of the walk, fresh out of training, in excellent physical shape, sharply dressed, and well-groomed. I was feeling on top of the world. I was definitely the man.

Rookie mistake. Black ice and rushing to the scene don't mix!

The ATM process was relatively new at the time, and a courtesy at these machines, which is common today, wasn't so common back then—at least not to dummies like me. That courtesy was to step back some distance so as not to make the customer in front of you nervous about you stealing his PIN—his personal identification number—or his money, for that matter.

A mature gentleman was at the machine. I was behind him, practically on his back. The lineup was about five or six people long. After inserting his card, the gentleman turned around, looked at me, and said, "Would you mind stepping back a bit?"

Today, I can't believe the words I blurted out back then. "You're safe with me, sir. I am a Mountie!"

Without a pause, he stared and me and replied, "Well, if you're a Mountie, you should know better!"

That was my first lesson as a Mountie in the real world. For an instant, I had forgotten who I really was and where I had come from. If somehow I could meet that gentleman today, I would surely thank him for putting me in my place. It was embarrassing at the time, but I heard his words. To this very day, if you see me at an ATM, I am the person standing about twenty-five feet behind the customer at the terminal.

Just a couple of days later, I was ready for my first shift, a brand new Mountie from small-town Newfoundland, and greener than fertilized lawns after a summer shower. My very first arrest seems very trivial now, but not so at the time.

My assigned trainer had picked me up. He was an awesome individual with whom I am still friends thirty-five years later. He had seven years' service and he had surely seen it all.

It was 6:00 p.m. on a Friday night, and only minutes into my first shift, when we received our first call from Dispatch. "Twenty-two Alpha Five. Dispatch."

My trainer told me to take it. This was my first call. My heart was already racing and I hadn't even heard the details yet.

I fumbled with the radio mic, and shyly, with a bit of a stutter, I replied, "Twenty-two Alpha Five here. Go ahead, Dispatch."

"Ten-four, we have a complaint that there are two intoxicated males causing a disturbance at the pizza takeout. The store owner wants them removed from the parking lot."

"Ten-four, Dispatch, copy that, we are ten-seventeen." Seventeen is the ten-code meaning that the officer or officers are en route to the location of the complaint.

This was not Depot anymore. This was real. I was stunned by the racing of my heart and the flush of nerves I felt. There was no getting out of this one, and these were not actors. My trainer rolled around the corner into the pizza takeout parking lot. I advised Dispatch, "Twenty-two Alpha Five is ten-seven scene."

Two young males, unsteady on their feet, were at the counter. My trainer said, "You take one, I'll take the other." Just like that. No planning, no practice, no rehearsing. It was not like Depot at all. I approached one of the men, who was so intoxicated I'm not even sure he realized that we were the police. It was obvious he needed to be taken to the drunk tank. I said to him, "You're under arrest for being intoxicated in a public place."

My trainer was already dragging his captive to the back seat of the police car. I followed with the mildly resistant drunk in tow. We conducted a brief search and secured both into the rear seat of the police car with doors securely locked. It was my first arrest. I got into the front passenger seat, and we drove off. The males started yelling and screaming. I was scared to death and frozen in place. Then, without warning, one of the drunks used his fist and punched the Plexiglas that divided the front and back seats. As he was behind me, I didn't see it coming. The smack reverberated loudly through the car, and I jumped. It scared the hell out of me. The only thing that stopped me from ejecting through the windshield was my seat belt. My trainer burst into laughter. He had to pull over to the shoulder to collect himself. I said to him, "That scared the shit out of me. That call actually made me nervous."

He laughed a little more and said, "That's good. When the time comes that a call like this doesn't make you nervous anymore, it's time to find a new job!" My trainer was an excellent police officer. Countless times he preached policies and procedures to me. I didn't always listen.

— Chapter 6 —

The Purple Slipper

In Canada, we have several hundred thousand laws that are all covered under the Ten Commandments.

Within the first few years of starting this job, and no longer under the watchful eye of my trainer, I attended the local shopping mall to address a complaint. The mall was filled with people, and as I walked to the location of the issue, I met a local person whom I had become acquainted with a few days earlier. As I approached her, she excitedly raised her arms above her head and said, "I didn't do it."

I thought, cute, original, and very funny, this person has a sense of humour. A few days later, I attended a complaint at a local bar. As I approached the entrance, a man whom I didn't know raised his arms above his head and claimed, "I didn't do it."

Twice in one week! What's with that? I thought.

As it turned out, I heard it dozens of times throughout the years. Each and every time, the speaker thought they were being original, funny, and unique. I was sick of hearing it, so much so that I feared that the next time I heard it, I would shoot the wannabe comedian. But I did hear it, again and again. Each time, I smiled and politely acknowledged the person's not-so-original attempt at humour. Each and every person believed they were the first. Maybe this time it would be my turn to say, "I didn't do it."

I was told that, generally, you need five years' experience on patrol before you're no longer considered a rookie. At only eight months' service, I was a super rookie, about to make a super rookie mistake.

I was working a night shift in a small town on the west coast of British Columbia. It was 3:00 a.m. and I had two hours left to complete my shift. At this time of the morning, the bars had just closed and most people were at home asleep. There remained a handful of stragglers roaming the empty streets, most of whom were either drunk or stoned, or both. The expected patrol duty at this hour of the morning was to round up impaired drivers, if possible. Police officers were also tasked with keeping an eye on businesses and such, to ensure no broken windows or kicked-in doors. We drive back and forth on the main streets, over and over, looking for oddities. High police visibility assists in the prevention of crime. The repetitive, slow drive back and forth on the streets is important. It's a huge deterrent to potential criminal activity, and it works. We used to call it "the sweep."

It was a warm July night, and the police dispatch radio was

really quiet. I drove slowly up and down the main drag of the town. The only other patrol car on duty at the time crawled by. The other officer gave me a thumbs-up. The only taxi in town had just pulled away from the bar with a carload of what hopefully were the last of the night owls. Once all was clear, we could return to the office to spend the last couple of hours completing the many pages of required paperwork.

I made what I hoped was one last sweep. I saw two guys walking along the sidewalk. They were clean-cut and well-dressed. There was no stumble or stagger in their walk. They gave me all the visual cues I needed to assure me that they were not troublemakers. Just to be sure, as I drove by, with my arm resting on the window frame, I gave them a small wave. That let them know that, "Hey, I see you." Any mischievous thoughts they might have had were now suppressed.

Another block or so would end the sweeps for the night. Soon the night shift would be over, I thought. I could go home and get some much-needed rest. Then a movement caught my eye in the left oncoming lane. Not on the sidewalk, but on the road. In the full illumination of my headlights, a young girl appeared. Her right arm was extended. Her tiny thumb was stuck out in the normal hitchhiking manner.

I say she was young, but I'm not really sure how old she was. She was at that age where you just couldn't tell. She may have been sixteen, or she may have been twenty-five. I didn't know. What I did know was that she was intoxicated—very intoxicated. She was tiny, about five feet tall, slim, with nice curves. She had long, messed-up blonde hair and a pretty face. She was barefoot, cradling two purple slippers under one arm. Maybe they were not slippers, but instead, some sort of new-style footwear that was hip at the time. They looked like slippers to me.

She was wearing tight blue cut-offs and a tight, white, flowery-collared blouse. But most important, it was obvious to me that she could barely walk. She almost collapsed at the knees with each struggled step.

I felt that this was a disaster waiting to happen. She could easily have been hit by a passing vehicle, or become a target for any pervert or socially deviant, intoxicated male.

It is a cardinal rule of police work not to pick up hitchhikers. For starters, it is against the law. Secondly, if you got in an accident and injured the hitchhiker, you were liable, both criminally and civilly. Third, there is the concern the hitchhiker might attempt some criminal act, such as grabbing the steering wheel. Finally, you may get an emergency call demanding your immediate attention. What would you do with the hitchhiker then?

In my rookie train of thought, I felt I was caught between a rock and a really hard place. If I drove by, how would I feel if she got run down, injured, or killed? What would happen the next day if I learned that she was targeted and sexually assaulted? So many horrible things could happen to a girl in such a state of intoxication at that time of the morning.

I immediately stopped the car. She stumbled to the driver's side and said, "Good day, Occifer."

I replied, "Do you have a ride or something? Where are you going?"

She slurred, "I'm staying with my friend down at Prak Road."

"You mean Park Road?"

"Yup, das it."

Park Road was about two kilometres away. She was not even close to Park Road, and she was walking in the wrong direction. There was no cab or other vehicle in sight.

I asked, "Can I call a cab, or something?"

"Got no money left," she replied.

Under the provincial liquor control act, I had authority to arrest her. Basically, the act states that any person found intoxicated in a public place can be arrested without a warrant. She was definitely intoxicated and in a public place. I could therefore legally arrest her and lock her up for her own protection. Yes, I would be in compliance with the act, but not with common practice. An arrest under this act was usually executed only if someone is intoxicated, is in a public place, and fits a third criteria not specified under the act. The subject must be committing some other disturbance, like yelling, screaming, being belligerent, or drunk to the point that they are lying almost comatose. This offence is designed to be used to arrest troublesome drunks. It de-escalates many situations. Yes, she was intoxicated, but not belligerent or causing a disturbance of any sort. I would not be making an arrest.

Instead, I decided to break the rules. Like, really, I asked myself, what could go wrong? So, I broke the rules and asked her, "Would you like a ride home?"

"Thank you," she said, and climbed into the back seat of my police car. She was still clinging to her purple slippers.

I felt a slight panic as I drove off. I was wondering what I would do with her if I got a call for service from Dispatch. What if the other patrol unit saw me? Would he rat me out for picking her up? I headed for Park Road. It seemed like a long drive. Then, headlights were coming toward me. Was it the other patrol car? I felt I was going to get caught. The vehicle approached, then slid by. It was a pickup truck.

Christ, that was close! I thought.

Almost there. She began to shout directions.

"That's it. Just there, the one with the brown fence."

I pulled off to the shoulder and stopped. The property was a small, cabin-style building, and the brown fence had an open gate. There was a light illuminating the porch. It did not appear that anybody was awake inside, as all the inside lights were out. It didn't matter, I thought. I got her there in one piece, safe and sound, and I did not get caught.

The back doors of the police car cannot be opened from the inside, obviously, so I exited the driver's-side door and opened her door to let her out.

"Thank you so much," she slurred, as she stumbled toward the house through the gate. I waited a second or two as she climbed up onto the porch.

I then drove off. I had broken one of the rules in our policies. I had done it to help someone out, and to my surprise, it felt good.

Upon returning to the office, I completed an hour or so of paperwork. The shift finally ended, and I could go home. Once I arrived home, I was exhausted and crawled into my bed and fell asleep almost instantly.

I was awakened abruptly as my wife shook me. It was nine in the morning. I had been asleep for all of just over three hours. I was still exhausted.

What the hell? I thought.

"The sergeant is at the door," my wife blurted out. "He said you have to go to the detachment. He won't tell me why."

Once the morning cobwebs cleared, I pulled on a pair of sweatpants and a T-shirt. With bad breath and dried crust in the corners of my eyes, I went to the door. The sergeant professionally said, "Get cleaned up. You have to come with me."

"What for?" I asked.

"Can't talk about it here. Just come with me."

My mind raced. I was confused. Someone saw me pick up the hitchhiker and ratted me out. I was screwed. I would lose my job. I quickly washed my face, brushed my teeth, slapped on a stroke of deodorant, and away I went.

Neither of us spoke en route to the detachment. I was scared. I could not have predicted that picking up a hitchhiker would hold such dire consequences.

We arrived at the detachment and the sergeant stated, "Let's go to my office."

The office clerk stared at me as I walked by. The day shift constable did not look up from his desk. He appeared abnormally busy with an abundance of paper in front of him.

Once I was inside the sergeant's office, he shut the door. "Sit down," he said.

"What's going on? What did I do?" I asked.

The sergeant looked away from me and calmly said, "It hurts me to do this, but I'm going to have to arrest you."

For a second I thought, *Okay, this is a joke.* He was arresting me for picking up a hitchhiker. Ha, ha, ha. But I wasn't finding it particularly funny, so I asked, "What for?"

"Sexual assault," he replied.

"What?" I was so taken aback, I was shouting.

"What did you do last night?' he asked.

Okay, I thought, I should confess my crime and tell the truth. So, I explained to him that I had picked up a hitchhiker. I drove a girl home for her own protection. "She was so drunk," I explained.

He then asked, "What else did you do?"

"Why are you asking such questions?" I was confused.

The sergeant then explained that there was a twenty-year-old girl at the hospital getting examined as a result of saying she had been raped. He explained that they had not had a chance to talk to her or get her statement. He informed me that she was picked up at six in the morning by a woman driving to work. After the woman picked her up and saw the crisis she was in, she took her to the hospital, and then the hospital called Dispatch to report the occurrence. The sergeant said that he had talked briefly to hospital staff and got a name and description of the girl. The girl was upset, and her attacker's details were scrambled. The hospital also noted she was wearing only one purple shoe.

"So, what's that got to do with me?" I asked.

The sergeant reached down to the floor behind the right side of his desk and lifted up a large clear evidence bag marked with date, time, location, and the sergeant's signature. The bag contained one purple slipper!

I was stunned and confused and almost didn't hear the sergeant say, "This was found on the floor of the patrol car you were driving last night." In shock, I replied, "Oh my God. You have got to be kidding me."

I was now fearful that the girl would not remember exactly what had transpired and possibly confuse me with her attacker. After all, she was extremely intoxicated. Would she mix me up with someone else? I wondered.

In a panicked and hurried fashion, I explained everything as it had occurred. The sergeant listened intently and compiled notes. He didn't seem overly convinced by my recollection of events. I was worried about what the girl's statement might say.

About an hour or so afterwards, while I sat quietly in the sergeant's office sipping a cup of black coffee, the on-duty officer picked up the victim and brought her to the office. The sergeant interviewed her for the details. It seemed like they were in the interview room for hours before he finally emerged. I could see him approach me, as I sat in his office, through the partially opened door. He stepped inside without closing the door.

"Well?" I anxiously asked.

He replied, "She tells me that she was picked up by a really nice police officer and that he gave her a ride. I presume that this nice police officer must be you."

I cracked a slight smile as the sergeant continued. "She said that after the officer dropped her off at her friend's, either no one was home or no one would answer the door. She tried to get into the house, but everything was locked up. She was not sure what to do, so she walked back out onto the road, and that was when a van stopped and she got inside. The driver took her to the gravel pit just off North Road, where he raped her, then let her go. She was smart enough to get the plate number. We know who it is."

I let out a sigh of relief.

As it turned out, when she exited my patrol car, I had failed to notice that she was no longer holding two purple slippers. Instead, she was holding just the one. The second was lying on the floor of my car.

Knowing the vehicle description and plate given by the victim, the day shift team picked up the suspect and arrested him within hours. An interview was conducted, and the suspect made a full confession. He blamed his actions on his drunken condition.

The sergeant apologized to me profusely, but also reminded me of the no-hitchhiker policy. I was free to go.

I never picked up another hitchhiker.

Time appeared to have stood still. I had time to think, and then, for no reason, the thought hit me. *What if he charges and I miss?* A gut-wrenching panic came over me. He was twenty feet away, and he could close that gap in a second. I get one shot. What if I miss? Over and over in my head, I wondered what I should do. I don't remember having felt like that at any other time. Was that fear? Feeling like having control of that situation, without having control of the situation? Having time to think like that, my stomach burning, and now several minutes in, a shiver started. No, this was not good at all.

"Come on, you shit pig, shoot me," he screamed. "What are ya waiting for?"

I had to get control. I had to stop the shivering. I had to fight against my body's natural reaction to this horribly stressful episode. What if I missed? I could not miss. I had been aiming with both arms extended in front of me, pointing instinctively as I had practised in training, over and over, so many times.

Pointing at centre mass, I had hit the practice targets with hundreds of rounds before, but now the situation was creating an uncertainty. During training, I may have struggled at swimming, but I had excelled at the firing range. The nine-millimetre semi-automatic pistol was loaded with fifteen rounds. I had lots of ammo, but he was so close that, if he charged, I would get only one shot. I should have been confident, but I wasn't. The adrenalin was triggering doubts as to my ability. I needed to take control. I needed to relax.

I yelled once more, "Burt, put down the damn knife! Let me help you."

My thoughts drifted back to more comforting days when I was the one in control. I wished my trainer had been there to assist me, as he surely would have known what to do.

Chapter 7

The Art of Training

The officer asked, "Are you drinking tonight?" The suspect replied, "Why are you asking? Are you buying?" They both had a good laugh, but the suspect still needed bail money!

A few years after breaking away from my trainer and carrying with me all the necessary skills I needed to be on my own, I eventually found myself in the reverse role as the trainer, with my own opportunity to teach and to share policing skills and, when the opportunity presented itself, to laugh at the expense of my own trainee. My first assignment was a nineteen-year-old kid from Ontario named Sean.

During our first few patrols, Sean was very anxious to prove himself. He wanted to show me his observational skills and all his newly acquired investigative techniques. As we drove around, he excitedly looked for things out of place and would make irrelevant comments about things, almost like a dog begging for a bone. I smiled inside at his innocence.

One afternoon while driving down this long rural road, we passed a car parked oddly on the shoulder of the road. To my surprise, Sean didn't say anything. A few seconds passed, and then I asked, "Sean, did you get the license plate of that vehicle? It's a good check out here in the middle of nowhere."

Sean had an expression of shit-I-missed-that-opportunity. In a panicked manoeuvre to redeem himself, he quickly rolled down the window and stuck his head out. He stretched his neck out past the door frame and looked back in an attempt to capture the plate number. Now with his head turned backwards to the wind, his sunglasses acted like a parachute and ripped from his head, crashing onto the highway behind us. He slumped back into the seat and looked at me.

"I am such a goof," he said.

He had the look of a scolded puppy. It was my turn to pull over to the shoulder and collect myself from laughing so much!

Sean was so eager and green that a good laugh at his expense was in order. I set into motion an elaborate prank. I told Sean that, because he was new in town, nobody knew him to be a police officer. I said that we had a bootlegger who sold beer after hours at a profit from his home. Unknown to Sean, the bootlegger would be one of our jail guards. The plan was for Sean to go to the bootlegger's residence with the cash, make the purchase, then return the contraband to the office. Sean would have a hidden microphone on him so I could monitor the transaction and ensure his safety. He had asked how he should pay for the goods, and I told him to use his own money. By doing this, afterwards, when we were done, I could teach him how to submit an expense claim to get his cash back. He was sold. Excited about his first potential catch, off he went.

A few minutes later, Sean arrived at the "suspect's" residence. The jail guard answered the door. Sean said he wanted to buy a flat of beer, the equivalent of twenty-four cans. The jail guard replied, "I don't know about this. You look like a cop to me."

Sean excitedly shouted back, "Nope, not me! No way."

"All right, then," the guard replied, "but I'm not sure about this one."

The exchange of beer for cash was made.

As he drove back to the office, the radio was filled with exuberance as Sean was blurting, "I got it, I did it, I made the buy! We get to arrest him. Yahoo!" He could not contain his excitement. Sean arrived at the office and was met with high-fives and congratulatory slaps. After all, he had just "taken down" our biggest bootlegger, whom we had been trying to arrest for months.

Now, what Sean didn't know was that there was a part two. I had arranged with Dispatch to send Sean and me on a fake call once the beer had been returned to the office. The call would take us to a rural part of town to deal with people allegedly driving dirt bikes on the roadway. Just moments later, the fake call was relayed to us by Dispatch, and Sean and

I were off. The beer was sitting on an office workstation desk. During this twenty minutes or so as Sean and I dealt with this dirt bike complaint, it was prearranged for off-duty members, including the jail guard, to scoop the beer from the office and bring it to the home of one of the off-duty members and enjoy a brew.

En route to the complaint, I asked Sean if he had secured his exhibit. He replied, "I left it on the table. Didn't you see it?"

Playing dumb, I suggested that the exhibit continuity was lost. "We can't use it in court. We can't arrest him," I said. I explained that an exhibit was an item seized relevant to a crime to be used as evidence against the accused. Tampering with an exhibit would get an officer suspended from the organization. So, Sean demanded, "Let's go back now and lock it up!"

Sean was worried, thinking he had fouled up what he thought was a perfect operation. When enough time had passed, we returned to the office. When we arrived there, Sean leaped from the police car and headed straight for his exhibit. It was gone! Sean ran from desk to desk, room to room, searching for his prize catch, but it was gone. He was sick. It didn't help that I reminded him how badly he had messed up. Then the office phone rang, right on cue, as planned. It was Constable Black inviting us to his house for coffee. Sean was despondent and didn't want to go, but under my command, he had no choice. Off we went, and we arrived at Constable Black's house a short time later. We rang the doorbell and were invited in. Sean couldn't believe his eyes as he entered the front room. Sitting around the table, sipping on what looked like his evidence, were four off-duty policemen, and the jail guard who had played the role of the bootlegger. The place broke out into a roar of laughter. Sean cracked a smile, but he was not getting it. He went into the adjacent room, and whispered, "Frank, come here."

Still laughing, I said, "What's wrong?"

"Frank, he's in there," he said.

"What do you mean?"

He replied, "The bootlegger is at the table. He's drinking the exhibit."

It hit me. Sean hadn't gotten it, so I explained, "Sean, that's the jail guard. We set you up. There is no bootlegger."

He let out a sigh of relief as the team enjoyed a cold beer, compliments of Sean.

During those days with Sean, I reiterated numerous dos and don'ts of police work. Some were important ones, like don't tamper with exhibits. Another important one was never to steal (obviously). I also reinforced what I thought was the most important trait of all: honesty. Always tell the truth—and yes, I reminded him never to pick up hitchhikers!

Throughout the years in police work, you did have the occasional opportunity to have a laugh or two, the majority of which were self-created. I didn't know it at the time, but I was told by a psychiatrist years later that this humour is created subconsciously as a coping mechanism for dealing with stress. I guess that's why police officers laugh at things that really are not all that funny. However, some humour is a result of misunderstanding.

"Sorry, ma'am, I thought this house was vacant!"

Later in my career, I was posted to the coast of Labrador. I had spent the last twenty or so years in British Columbia and had forgotten a lot of Newfoundland dialects.

While on duty one afternoon, I received a call that I did not quite understand. The caller stated that her neighbour's dog was clear. Not knowing what this meant, I called the complainant to get the facts. The call went something like this:

"Hello. I understand you have a problem and need the police?"

"Yes, the neighbour's dog is clear, and I am sick of it," replied the caller.

I said, "What exactly is the dog doing, and when you say 'clear,' do you mean he is white, or similar to a yellow lab?"

The caller replied, "No, that is what he is doing, he is clear, you know, he is roaming free."

I then understood what "clear" meant. It meant the dog was not on a leash or tether. It was an expression I had not heard before.

I replied to her, "Okay, so you're saying the dog is at large?"

"No, b'y," she replied. "He's not that big. He's just a little dog. You're some stunned!"

I did know, however, that "stunned" was a Newfoundland expression for stupid!

A few days later, there was another call. "The young fellas are smoking pot on the bridge."

I quickly drove to the only bridge in town. There was nobody there, so I assumed they had left. I returned to the office and called the complainant to advise of the actions I had taken. That call went something like this:

"Thank you for your call, but I went to the bridge and there was nobody there."

The caller responded, "How can that be? They are still there smoking pot! I can see them from my window."

Now I was confused. "Well, there's only one bridge in town, and believe me, there is no one on it."

The caller stated, "What? Just about every second house has a bridge. You didn't go to the right house."

Stupidly, I replied, "How can every second house have a bridge? They just have driveways."

The caller, now getting impatient, said, "No, b'y, the bridge on the back of the house. You know, the dick."

It hit me: the "dick" is a deck, and a deck is a bridge. Yes, I am stunned!

Just when I thought I had all the accents and dialects figured out, I got struck once again. I attended a break-in at a residence on a late Saturday afternoon. After I had looked around to ensure the home was safe and secure, I requested a statement from the homeowner relevant to what was stolen. The caller said that she needed to go through everything and come to the office with the list on Monday. I wouldn't be working Monday, but I would be working the next day, Sunday, so I asked her, "Can you bring the list in tomorrow?"

She replied, "I can't come in on Sunday. My face is very important to me."

Now, she was not a model or anything, but as a professional, I had to respect her concerns. The fact that her face was important to her didn't really make any sense, and I didn't know why it would prevent her from bringing in the list on Sunday. I wasn't sure what to say without insulting her, so I said, "Well, my face is important to me, too. But I don't understand why you can't bring it in on Sunday."

She replied, "Not my face, my faith. My faith, b'y. I don't do stuff on Sunday."

Yup! I am really stunned!

As good a laugh as that was, I'll never forget those days on the coast of Labrador. This was a place where I had the pleasure of meeting some of the most gentle and salt-of-the-earth people anywhere. The time I spent there helped to restore my faith in humanity!

Unfortunately, the fun times in the police environment are rare. It is mostly all work and no play. Sometimes it was intriguing, as was the first case I had experienced involving a search relative to a murder. I was shocked by what lengths some investigators would go to in order to bring closure to a case.

— Chapter 8 —

A Baseball Bat

If you really want to conquer something, you will find a way. If you do not, you will find an excuse.

Tony was thirty years old, and his best friend, George, was twenty-nine. Tony had an eleven-year-old girl named Joan. One evening while Tony and George were partying, Tony passed out from overindulgence of alcohol. This provided George with an opportunity, and in his drunken state, he raped little Joan. When he had finished, he left the residence. Joan was extremely traumatized but had the wits to call 911. It didn't take police long to locate and arrest George. The case was solid. Joan's recollection was remarkably sound, and the medical professionals confirmed her allegations. DNA was also collected and preserved to solidify the case even further. George was released on bail, as he had no prior criminal convictions.

Several weeks later, George was found dead in a ditch on the side of the highway. His injuries appeared to be the result of multiple blunt force traumas to the back of his head, neck, and shoulders. It was evident that he had been struck from behind by a vehicle. We were investigating a hit and run.

I recall driving miles and miles, one driveway at a time, looking for a vehicle with new front-end damage. The hit-and-run investigation continued for two days, until the forensic medical examiner provided news that sent a shock through the community. It was not a hit and run. Upon examination, it was revealed that his injuries were the result of being struck multiple times with a long, round object, similar to a pipe or baseball bat. Someone had come up behind George as he was walking and struck him with a pipe or something similar. George had been beaten to death.

As investigators, we backed up, reorganized ourselves, and changed direction. It wasn't long after that a witness, who had been at the local bar, recalled overhearing a man talking about how he was pissed off about George raping a young girl. The man who was doing the talking was eventually identified as Joan's uncle. He was asked to attend the office for questioning, and did so. Following an intense interrogation, he eventually admitted to committing the crime. He said he was so upset about his niece being raped that he thought he was justified in doing what he did. He took the law into his own hands and beat George from behind with a baseball bat. When the uncle had left George in the ditch, he said he wasn't sure if he was dead or still alive. When he was asked about the baseball bat, he said he drove to the beach and threw it into the ocean.

A murder weapon can be a critical piece of evidence to support a criminal case. Although the case was solid, it is customary to pursue all potential evidence and leave no stone unturned, so an effort had to be made to find the baseball bat. The fact that it had been tossed into the ocean several weeks before was a major obstacle. I was about to witness a remarkable investigative effort, unlike anything I had ever seen before.

An officer from our marine section offered his expertise. He gathered maps of the area and ocean current flow data from Environment Canada. He also gathered information on weather and wind conditions from the date the baseball bat was tossed. Using all the data, he processed and carefully estimated that an object like a baseball bat would ultimately wash ashore on a certain date at an approximate location. The date he proposed had just passed, and the location was twenty-seven kilometres away, in a small inlet. Despite having doubts, a team headed out to search the area.

The other searchers and I were all thinking the same thing. Our chances of finding the bat were slim. Even if the bat was in the area identified by the marine section member, how could anyone possibly see it? The beaches were strewn with layers of washed-up kelp, logs—lots of logs—dead jellyfish, and garbage from the hundreds of boats that cruised that popular sound daily. Regardless, once we arrived, the search began.

After a couple of hours of searching, it was evident that our efforts were a lost cause. The bat could not be found. The criminal case would have to be pursued without the weapon. After a brief discussion, it was decided we would search until 3:00 p.m. and then call it off. That was only twenty minutes more.

Shortly before three, one of our searchers decided he was done. He stopped, gave up, and decided it was a failure. He reached into his pocket and pulled out a Snickers chocolate bar and had a little snack. As he was finishing the last few bites, he accidentally dropped the wrapper onto the ground. He bent over to pick it up and noticed something that caught his eye. He kicked away a log, shifted some kelp to the side, and astonishingly, the baseball bat was lying amidst the litter! Amazingly, the bat still possessed particles of the victim's DNA. Joan's uncle was convicted of manslaughter and spent seven years in jail.

That was certainly a lesson in perseverance. Then something even more shocking occurred in my career. I never knew that one's perceived observations could be so far removed from actual fact.

— Chapter 9 —

Seeing and Believing

Just because it has a perfectly articulated scientific explanation does not mean it is not a miracle.

It was 1984, in northern British Columbia. It was a beautiful summer day with crystal clear blue skies, and a temperature of thirty degrees Celsius. I was on patrol around a small rural town, and music filled the Suburban police vehicle. It was a quiet day, and most folks were enjoying the weather this day, a rare reprieve from a long, cold winter. Sometime around noon, a call came over the police radio

"Five Bravo two, Telecoms."

"Five Bravo two, here, go ahead."

"What's your twenty?"

"Just here in town."

"We have a complaint north on King Creek Road. Is there another unit closer to that location?"

"Ah, I'm the only one on shift right now."

"Ten-four. I was hoping someone was closer. We have a report of a vehicle rollover at approximately the seventy-kilometre mark on King Creek Road. Unknown if there are any injuries. Details are vague. An ambulance has been dispatched."

"Ten-four. I'm en route. Advise if further info comes in."

"Ten-four."

I turned the Suburban around, activated the lights and siren, and began the seventy-kilometre journey on a narrow, winding, dusty, and pothole-pitted gravel road. It would take thirty minutes to get there, with lots of time to plan for the task ahead. It was possible that, by the time I got there, someone may have given the involved persons a ride to their homes and I merely needed to retrieve an ownership registration and take a few photos for any potential insurance claim.

As I had figured, I rolled onto the scene in about thirty minutes and radioed my arrival.

"Dispatch, I am ten-seven scene."

No ambulance had arrived yet. A few logging trucks had pulled over to the side of the road to lend assistance. The accident was on a corner. The wheel impressions in the gravel told a story of a two-wheel-drive, older Ford truck approaching a corner at too high a speed. It was suggested from the skid marks that the driver may have locked the brakes, sending the vehicle into a spin. The driver of the vehicle probably lost control, flipping several times before crashing into some rocks. The crash tossed all contents, including the unbelted occupants, into the local terrain.

I was not expecting this. Dispatch had said there was an accident, but they hadn't said that there were fatalities. However, Dispatch was to be forgiven, as they only relayed what they had known, nothing more.

Nevertheless, I'd had a lot of experience, and this wasn't anything I hadn't seen before. Or so I thought.

My first order of business was to determine if there were any survivors, or anyone needing medical care. It took only seconds to realize that no medical help was needed. The driver was a young mother, approximately twenty-five years of age. Her mangled remains, blood-soaked clothing, and awkwardly twisted neck left me no doubt that she was deceased. Lying several feet from her was what I presumed to be her son, about four or five years old, and he was also deceased. I observed a small green tarp covering another body, and I wasn't sure why this one was covered. One of the truck drivers explained that he had covered this one up. His words to me were, "Just too hard to look at, so I put a tarp over the body."

I asked, "Male or female?"

He replied, "Looks like a young girl."

I could hear the siren from the ambulance getting closer. *Good, lots of help*, I thought.

I proceeded to get witness details and learned there were no witnesses to the crash. It was evident that the truck drivers had come upon the scene after the fact. I took names and details as best I could gather, and then began the photos. I took about six pictures of the red Ford pickup from every angle, then photographed the bodies. I wrote the details in my notebook as I went, step by step, systematically, the mother first, the son second. I snapped full body pictures, then close-ups showing visible injuries, then facials for identification. Finally, it was time to face the green tarp.

I gently removed the tarp, and underneath was a beautiful young girl whom I figured was three or four years old. She had blonde hair and was wearing a very light flower-patterned summer dress and one sock. The other sock and both shoes were located farther down the road. I remember thinking what a pretty young girl she was and wondering how she had died. It appeared that she had no injuries at all. By now the ambulance had arrived and the paramedics were standing at my side. I remarked, "Strange that she's gone. Looks like she's just lying there having a nap."

The paramedic looked at me strangely, but I didn't know why at the time.

I finished up my photos.

Eventually the scene investigation was completed, with everything done. The ambulance transported the unfortunates, and I returned to the office.

Back then there was no digital photography. The procedure was to use film, and the film was sent to the RCMP laboratory in Ottawa for processing and then returned to the investigator for placement on file. I received my photos back about three weeks later, which was standard at the time. Normally the photos were tagged and placed on the police file, but before doing so, I usually took a quick look at them.

I opened the photo pack, and the first photo I viewed was that of the truck. It was a picture of a blue Ford! My initial reaction was, shit, Ottawa had sent me photos from someone else's collision scene, as my truck was red. The next photo was that of the woman, which was accurate from the photo I had remembered taking of her. Then the young boy. All appeared accurate, and then, finally, I viewed the photo of the young girl. I was horrified.

The photo that I had taken of the pretty young girl sleeping was a picture showing a girl at the same location, same dress and same posture as my girl. However, this girl had a severe blunt force trauma laceration from hitting a sharp rock. The laceration started at her forehead and ended at her throat. Her head had literally been split open.

Ottawa had not made a mistake. These were my photos, and I had not seen this. My red truck was, factually, blue. As for the girl's injury, I had not seen it. My subconscious had blocked it out. I know now why the paramedic looked at me strangely when I suggested she looked like she was having a nap. I didn't understand or comprehend why I had not seen the images for what they were. I will never know for certain why. I can only surmise that some metabolic safety trigger, something subconscious, had blocked what was real. Thirty years later, as I look back, I would still swear that my own observations were more accurate than the photos, but I know that it is not true.

What was happening with Burt was true. He was swinging a machete. For some reason, I then became scared that I would miss him if I shot at him with my firearm. I was suffering from a lack of confidence, which I had to overcome. I closed one eye, and ever so slowly, I raised my pistol away from his centre mass. I sighted down the short barrel with my eye. I locked my sightline onto his chest and moved up over his unshaven, frothing mouth, over his snot-dripping nose, and stopped directly between his bloodshot eyes. I stopped here. There was new confidence. I was not going to miss.

Despite his rage, his yelling, and his drunken condition, when I did this, I saw something. He flinched, ever so slightly, but he flinched. It was only now that he realized I was totally serious. I was not going to miss! Now more questions raced through my mind. If he wanted me to kill him now, why had he flinched? Why should it bother him? Was it really his wish to die? I had stopped shivering. I was in control. I tried talking to him.

"Burt, you are being silly. Drop the knife and we can sort this out. I can get you some help."

For the first time I saw a new look on his face, a look that cried, *What the hell am I doing here?*

Then more questions. Would this end in murder? How could I resolve this? The standoff had lasted only minutes, but already it had seemed like a very long day.

— Chapter 10 —

Some Long Days

There is an old expression that states, "The Mounties always get their man." Sure, in the real world this would be nice, but unfortunately, it is simply not true.

My sheltered upbringing and the innocence of my youth did not prepare me for my first murder case, or the others that followed. Murder was something that I had never given any thought to. It wasn't part of the life that I knew. In fact, I don't even recall ever hearing the word in my youth.

In training, during lectures dealing with murder and investigations, it hadn't hit me that humans kill each other. It was kind of like those classes were just part of the curriculum that needed to be covered, but never anything that I would need. I had a nonchalant attitude about the whole subject. In the real world, that would change, real fast. This new experience would bring with it a whole spectrum of emotions that tore away at my conscience. Even now, years later, as I think about them, the same stir of emotions rips through me.

For those who are unaware, the Criminal Code has various offences that may be considered when a person dies at the hands of another. They are the offences of first-degree murder, second-degree murder, and manslaughter. The elements that comprise the various offences can be varied and complex.

To explain in the simplest terms, first-degree murder occurs when the event was planned and deliberate. As an example, a man learns that his wife is having an affair. He does not act immediately, but instead takes some time and plans a strategic method to murder her. Once all his careful planning is in place, he commits the murder. The accused had intended to carry out this crime. A conviction for first-degree murder will fetch the accused life imprisonment with no eligibility for parole for twenty-five years.

In the case of second-degree murder, the same man comes home early from work and catches his wife in bed with another man. A fight ensues. The husband is in such a fit of jealousy and anger, he kills the other man—and meant to kill him—but he had not planned it. It just happened, unplanned. Second-degree murder is considered less serious. Thus, a conviction generally means parole eligibility is improved.

Manslaughter is when the same man comes home early from work and catches his wife on the couch with another man. The husband grabs him, and in a fit of sudden rage, he punches him. The punch knocks the victim backwards, and as he stumbles, he strikes his head on the coffee table, causing blunt force trauma to the skull resulting in his death. The husband was not trying to murder him and had no intent, nor a plan. However, his actions resulted in the death of the other man. Thus, manslaughter applies. A conviction for manslaughter is once again far less serious than the previous two offences.

The best training in the world cannot prepare police officers for their first murder case.

Amy's family was vacationing at a small lakeside cabin. Her mother was only twenty-two years old and her father was twenty-five. Little Amy was only three years old. It was a very warm summer night, so when the family bunked down for the night, they left the sliding door facing the water open to help keep everyone cool. The sliding door had a built-in screen slider to contend with the bugs. There was no air conditioning. Amy's mother and father fell fast asleep in the one-bedroom cabin. Little Amy was happy with a blanket on the couch in the main living area.

About 5:00 a.m., Amy's mom awoke to go to the bathroom, and while up, she checked on Amy. The sliding screen door was open. Amy was not on the couch. That's when our police office got the call.

I arrived at the office prepared for another normal shift at 8:00 a.m. When I saw the collection of various vehicles in the parking lot, I knew something was amiss. The debriefing that followed shortly thereafter informed everyone present of the occurrence. Our members who had been called out earlier were on scene, and the search for a missing child had already begun.

I was assigned the role of file manager. My task was to create a file and add all investigative information to that file as it was received—not a difficult task, considering we were dealing with a missing child. All were confident that she would be found in hours.

Those hours turned into days—seven, to be exact. The previous week had seen several theories crash and burn. As an example, Amy was known to sleepwalk. It was theorized that she had slipped through the screen door in the early morning hours and went into the lake. However, police divers ruled out that theory. Day seven would change things dramatically.

A young couple hiking through a park miles away in another community sat on a fallen log to have a rest and a snack. They noticed a peculiar odour. A quick search through some nearby brush revealed Amy's body.

The missing person file was now a murder investigation. Amy had been raped and strangled.

There was very little evidence to pursue from an investigative angle. A few days passed, and there was a massive media frenzy. This prompted a young man to come to our office. In a statement that he provided, he said he knew who the murderer was. It was his eighteen-year-old male friend.

As a result of his information, a suspect was arrested, charged, and convicted of second-degree murder. He sits in jail to this day. He killed her because he didn't want her to tell anyone that he'd had sex with her. She was only three years old. It horrified me that someone would kill a child for sex. It was a new lesson for me as to what some humans could do.

Sandra was sixteen years old. She was last seen hitchhiking on a busy provincial highway. There were no witnesses who could assist in identifying a vehicle that may have picked her up. Sandra was a missing person file, with no leads. An exhaustive missing person investigation was carried out and generated no evidence. Approximately two weeks later, Sandra's badly decomposed body was found on an abandoned logging road. The autopsy that followed revealed that she had been raped, then strangled with a rope. What was a missing person file was now another murder case.

Thousands of tips were investigated over the next few years in an attempt to solve the crime. No arrest was ever made. Sadly, her murderer remains unidentified, and Sandra's file now sits in a cold case box. We had failed her.

Tony was a drifter who moved to an isolated community. One day he stumbled upon an outdoor marijuana grow operation and decided to help himself. What occurred next was a complete mystery, and now, years later, Tony's is a very cold case. It was suspected that the owners of the marijuana crop happened to visit the growing site at the same time as Tony was there and didn't take kindly to Tony having helped himself to some of the crop. The only evidence we had to help investigate this was a piece of jawbone found at the scene. DNA was extracted and used to identify Tony. Although nothing was ever proven, it was theorized that the grow operation owners caught him, roped him to a tree, and shot him in the head at point-blank range. No other body parts were ever found. There were no witnesses or evidence to assist in the investigation. We failed Tony, also.

Devon was eccentric, to say the least. At thirty years of age, he had moved from the city to this small town in northern British Columbia. He was a self-proclaimed martial artist and joined the local gym where he could go and practise. Four local lads took a dislike to him and challenged him to fight on many occasions. Each time, Devon declined. He had no interest in practising his martial art skills on four immature teens.

The young lads continued to harass and provoke Devon, until one day he snapped. With a loaded shotgun, Devon drove around the small town until he located the lads. It didn't take much for Devon to provoke the boys into following his vehicle and taunting Devon even more. This encounter resulted in both vehicles travelling to a secluded area on the edge of town. At road's end, the lads stopped and stepped out of the vehicle, prepared to see just how good Devon's martial art skills were. They were ready to lay a beating on him.

For reasons we may never know, Devon stepped from his vehicle with the shotgun and opened fire. He blew all four youths away. Three died instantly. The fourth miraculously survived, despite a shotgun blast to the torso. Devon escaped the scene. A witness in the area had heard the four blasts of the shotgun and called police immediately. Police arrived on the grisly scene within minutes. It wasn't long before they learned the suspect was Devon. A manhunt began. It included police dogs, helicopters, infrared equipment, divers, and dozens of policemen. The search lasted for years, but Devon was never found and remains at large today. We had failed again.

These failures not only hurt the families, friends, and loved ones involved, but they hurt the police personnel, also. The failures diminished their confidence and damaged their public image. Simply put, it just hurts to fail.

Fortunately, a police officer's sanity occasionally gets spared, as not all police work is serious. Once in a while you meet someone who presents you with an opportunity to have a little fun.

— Chapter 11 —

The Toothache

Be careful what you practise.
You may get good at the wrong thing.

Jimmy meant well, but he always managed to get himself in trouble with the law. The best way to describe him would be to say that he was like a ship with a powerful engine, but somewhere along the way, the rudder fell off. He was well-known to police, but never for anything outrageous. He was a busy man, to say the least.

One hot Friday afternoon in July, Jimmy was drunk, again. He entered the local grocery store and lifted two steaks. A store clerk watched him as he stuffed them inside the front of his shirt and left the store without paying. Wisely, the clerk did not confront him, but instead called the police.

Sam and I answered the call. We first went to the grocery store to confirm the details with the store clerk, and there was no mistaking that the suspect was Jimmy and that he had stolen two steaks valued at $12. Once a statement was taken from the store clerk, we headed to Jimmy's place. In the twenty minutes or so that had elapsed since the occurrence, he was only now getting home. I could see a bulge under his shirt. I asked him if he was at the store, and he replied, "Nope."

I said, "I think you were, and I believe you stole two pork chops." I threw in the change of meat description on a whim, just to see what he would say.

To my surprise, he suddenly looked confused, then reached into the front of his shirt. Pulling out his loot, he studied it and said, "This is not pork chops, it's steak." Jimmy's rudder was still broken.

I arrested Jimmy for theft, and because he was intoxicated and had a history of such thefts, we had to take him to jail.

I asked him to get into the police car, just as I had done on at least five occasions before this, but this time he resisted. He didn't punch or kick, but he really resisted, which was something he had never done before. Sam and I dragged, pushed, and pulled him up the driveway to the car, and he battled us the whole way. He never said a word, just grunted and groaned until he ran out of breath. Finally at the car, he would not get in. He braced each hand against the frame and was not going in. Sam and I were getting exhausted from the fight. We finally managed to break his hands free, and he was cast head first into the back seat and the door was slammed shut. I'm not sure what got into him; he had never done that before. I thought it was over, and I was feeling fortunate that Jimmy was finally detained without any harm to anyone.

Once inside the prisoner bay at the detachment, we opened the back car door to remove Jimmy. The battle was on again. He would not get out. He fought and wrestled and resisted the whole way, again not punching or kicking, but resisting and being a nuisance. From the moment we got him out of the police vehicle, through the prisoner bay, and down the long hall to the jail cell, he never stopped fighting for an instant. Finally, he was held against the wall, searched, and pushed into the cell. Sam and I were exhausted. Sweat was pouring from our faces, and we were both angry. Now sitting in the jail cell, Jimmy began a roaring melody. It was out of tune, but it was the unmistakable classic written back in the 1960s by Sonny Curtis of the Crickets. "I fought the law and the law won. I fought the law and the law wonnnn!" And again, "I fought the law and the law won, I fought the law and the law wonnnnnn!" Sam and I broke into such laughter that our stomachs hurt.

Due to Jimmy's history, we obtained the endorsement of a Justice of the Peace, and he was held for court until Monday. It was going to be a long weekend for Jimmy.

Saturday afternoon, Jimmy began crying about a toothache. We ignored it, assuming it was a scam to get himself released. On Sunday morning, he was reeling in pain. His lower cheek was swollen, and it was obvious that he was not faking. The local dentist just happened to be a friend of ours, and Sam saw this as an opportunity to have a little fun. We escorted Jimmy to the dentist, who had unlocked his facility just for us. The dentist went through his routine, and an examination quickly revealed that an extraction was necessary due to a decayed molar. The doctor injected the anaesthetic.

Meanwhile, as I was watching over Jimmy, Sam slipped out and dropped by the local wildlife office. He gathered himself a moose tooth from one of the seized specimens and returned with the tooth to the dental office. Once Jimmy's jaw was sufficiently numb, the dentist yanked and pulled the molar from Jimmy's jaw. As the doctor held it over the stainless steel tray, Sam dropped the moose tooth and—*clunk!*—it landed in the tray. The dentist quietly slipped the real tooth into the garbage. The size of the hole left by the extracted molar required sutures. The dentist soon finished up, and finally Jimmy could return to the jail cell. Then Jimmy asked, as everyone does, if he could see the tooth. The dentist picked up the moose tooth with his pinchers.

Jimmy gasped. "It's freaking huge!"

The dentist responded, "Yup. Most of it was below the gum. That's why it hurt so much!"

Then, also just like everyone else who visits a dentist, Jimmy asked, "Can I keep it?"

"Absolutely!" replied the dentist, and Jimmy collected his prize molar. Jimmy had no idea why we were all laughing so hard. He carried that tooth with him everywhere and showed it off at every opportunity. Sporting his prize molar, he was quickly dubbed Jimmy the Jaw by his friends and associates.

The standoff continued. Burt had not relented. The taunting with the machete and the rants for me to kill him persisted.

I thought, if he really wanted to die, why hadn't he just stepped forward? That would have made my decision much easier. But no, he held his ground and continued to rant.

The fun days now seemed so far away. This real world was just not that much fun. There was lots of time to think, *Will I die? Maybe God will save me.*

I have never been sure that God as the biblical character is portrayed exists, but I have always believed in something. I can't describe it, I can't explain it, and I don't know what it looks like or where it is, but I have no doubt that somewhere, somehow, there exists a greater entity. I don't know if it is a power, a force, or a being, but it is commonly called God, and for a millennium, God has explained that which cannot be explained.

— Chapter 12 —

Little Red Cross

So many people travel the world and are amazed at the vastness of the oceans—they are astonished at the magnificence of the mountains and hypnotized by the beauty of a sunset—yet they never take a look at themselves and wonder.

The community of Freshwater on Bell Island, Newfoundland, is about as remote as it gets, but occasionally it can be a special place. In this rural part of the world, when I was a young boy, I had but one close neighbour, an older man named Arthur Parsons. Although he was no relation at all, out of respect way back then we were taught to call older people Uncle or Aunt. He was called Uncle Arthur, and he lived with his lovely wife, Aunt Lucy.

I was but a mere eight years old and had developed a desire to work with wood. Uncle Arthur provided me an opportunity to explore this desire in his workshop. It wasn't much, just a small eight-foot-by-ten-foot shed with the bare essentials—a wooden-handled hammer, a rusty hand saw, an old block plane, a bench-mounted vise, an auger, and some bits. Uncle Arthur was a short man, about five feet and four inches. He was always neatly groomed, had no facial hair, and he had two hats. He always wore his clean and tidy hat on Sunday, and the tattered and worn old felt hat that he wore every other day. He always wore pants that were held up by suspenders. For shirts he favoured plaid. I would spend many hours around this old man, picking up bits and pieces of his vast knowledge. He was almost a father figure to replace the father I had lost.

Uncle Arthur was of strong Protestant faith, so much so that I thought the perfect woodworking gift for him would be a wooden Cross. So, with two small sticks, I carved away at this Cross for many hours. However, to make it more than just another ordinary Cross, I cut out the middle section of each of the two sticks to make a perfect halved joint. With a little sanding, a piece of wooden magic was born. I presented it to Uncle Arthur, and he was thrilled to receive this surprise gift.

He was so surprised that he felt it deserved special attention, so he dug out a small can of red paint and proceeded to paint what became his little red Cross. He then drove a tiny nail into the top, where he tied a small braided twine. Once he had picked a spot for it, he decided he was going to hang it with the tiny loop that he had tied into the twine. He fetched his old ink-filled quill and proceeded to inscribe the words "Made by Frankie Pitts, Easter, 1967."

He was so proud of this Cross that he hung it at the entrance to his house, just inside the porch, in a prominent spot by the door casing, so that no one could enter without seeing it. I was thrilled. Over the years, I walked by it a thousand times as Aunt Lucy would invite me in for snacks on occasion. There was always tea and some "bickies," as we Newfoundlanders called biscuits. The Cross hung in that little spot for years.

Then, as with all things, life went on and I moved away from home at the age of sixteen. Days became weeks, weeks became years, and my thoughts often went back to those early days. My new RCMP career, which started when I was twenty-two, required me to move to British Columbia, many miles away. I pretty much lost all touch with those who were such an integral part of my youth, including Uncle Arthur. I often thought of the Cross and wondered what had happened to it. Sometime during those disconnected years, I heard that Aunt Lucy had sadly passed, but I don't recall the date. Uncle Arthur followed soon afterwards. When I heard the news of his passing, I remembered thinking how selfish it was of me to have lost touch over the years with a man and woman who were such a special part of my youth.

Following his passing, his house was sold to an American fellow who wanted to use it as a summer home. That plan failed, for whatever reason, and the house changed hands again. A local person bought it and tore out the interior for a massive renovation. No doubt the Cross had been lost in the dust, that is, if it even survived the American adventure. Following the renovation, I learned that the house had become a rental with tenants unknown to me, and as before, this was another failed venture, resulting in the place once again being sold to another older couple.

Many years passed, and I often wondered about the Cross, and how I should have rescued it upon hearing of Uncle Arthur's passing. But such is life, and like most people, I moved on. Sad indeed that the little red Cross I had created so many years before had been lost.

In 2005, almost forty years after I delighted Uncle Arthur with the little woodworking gift, I was on a summer vacation and had returned to that little spot on earth where I had grown up. It was a beautiful and warm August day. My first stop during this trip was to see my father's grave. After parking the car, I walked up past the old white church to the graveyard. My father's grave was located about halfway up the first row. It was overgrown, and the headstone had faded. A cascade of emotions suddenly engulfed me. All these years had passed, and now I had been cast back to the very day the box was buried. My throat swelled, and I could not hold back the tears. I looked away, only to see the graves of Uncle Arthur and Aunt Lucy. I knew them all. There lay my childhood friend Ronnie. He had been taken far too young, and I hadn't realized that he had been buried here. It seemed that everyone from my youth was gathered in this one little spot on the side of a small hill. I looked again to my father's grave. I could see the box being lowered, the image as perfect as the day it had happened. Through tears, I said a prayer and left. I couldn't stay. I had to get out of there, so I drove away, feeling sad, realizing just how short this journey called life really is.

After a brief drive and several tissues, I was ready for my next stop. I parked my car and began walking around where so many years ago I used to run. I could smell the vast open hayfields that lined the gently rolling hills. There appeared to be no one around, so I had the land all to myself. Warm memories brought tears as I reminisced over things from my youth.

I walked by Uncle Arthur's house. It was not even recognizable now, due to the renovations the various owners had implemented. I stood there pondering the fragile balance of life, the meaning of it all. Then, almost as if it was orchestrated, an older lady emerged from the porch of the house and said, "Good day."

I replied to her, and we exchanged subdued greetings. We talked about how everyone had moved away, about the beautiful warm day, and how quiet it was. Then she asked me what I was doing. I told her that I had grown up here, and pointed to the old abandoned shack that used to be my home. I told her my name was Frank Pitts and that I was just visiting, wandering around and enjoying the day. When I told her my name, a warm smile came over her face, and she said, "Wait right here. I have something to show you."

She disappeared into the house and emerged a few minutes later. She walked up to me and opened her hand. Unbelievably, like a blessing from heaven, she was holding my little red Cross. I was delighted, and amazed! My tears became a river as a flood of emotion surged through me. She told me she had found it in a garbage pile many years ago, picked it up, and put it away. She said that when she saw it, she knew that one day she would return it to me. Her name was Aggie.

"Made by Frankie Pitts. Easter - 1967."

Sadly, she died three years later. I pray she made it to heaven! I hung my Cross in a prominent spot inside my home, just as Uncle Arthur had done, still bound by the very string that

Uncle Arthur had attached so many years before. Just a mere coincidence? I do not believe that.

And now this. A man was begging me to kill him. I had to figure out how to get out of this so that we could all go home without anyone being hurt. Maybe that greater power would intervene. I had seen things before that have had no other explanation than some sort of supernatural intervention.

— Chapter 13 —

A Tragic Disappearance

Human beings can survive a week without water, two weeks without food, and years without a home. Remove the police, and see just how long they would last.

It was a cold October day in 1985, in a community on the southwest coast of British Columbia. This Saturday, although cold, was very sunny, which is often the case in the fall of the year in this corner of the planet. It was perfect weather for blackberry picking, which is where this incredible story begins.

I was a young constable at the time, and at about 1400 hours—police talk for 2:00 p.m.—I received a call from a distraught elderly gentleman who stated that his wife was missing. I hurried to the address he provided. It was a rural area with no adjacent neighbours, but instead a large acreage with lots of trees and blackberry bushes. Blackberries grew abundantly here, and the growing season was very conducive to a rich supply of these tasty little berries. Once I arrived, the gentleman explained that his wife, Mrs. Burke, had gone outside with a bowl to pick some blackberries. When she didn't return, her husband panicked and went looking for her but could not find her. He did find her eyeglasses, lying on the ground beside a white bowl that contained a couple of cups of berries. There were no other signs to help figure out where she might have gone.

Her husband was crying and very distraught. In the interview that followed, I learned that, without her eyeglasses, his wife was legally blind. She was a diabetic who required insulin. She also had high blood pressure requiring medication, and she was recently diagnosed with early stages of Alzheimer's disease. To complicate matters even more, this lady was eighty-five years old.

A preliminary perimeter search turned up nothing. She had totally disappeared, and considering her health problems, it was unlikely she would survive the night. Search and rescue were called to avail of the few hours of daylight left. The police dog was put to work, as well as the police helicopter. The day eventually ended and turned into night. Volunteers arrived with flashlights, determined on finding this poor old gal. Her husband was not coping well with her disappearance. Sunday brought another fine day for searching, and I was up early, helping with the organizing. I was now thinking that we would find a body. Her survival odds were remote as it was cold and she did not have any food, nor even a warm sweater. Sunday's vigorous search turned up nothing.

New theories surfaced. One such theory was that she was carried off by a cougar, which did happen in that part of the world. Another suggested a grizzly bear attack, and yet others rumoured that her husband murdered her and stashed the body. Yes, people were talking, but all evidence led to the fact that she simply went berry picking close to home and never came back.

Monday's search was as intense as the day before, although most searchers were now resigned to the fact that they would find a body, or maybe just some clothing. It had been so long now that most bets were that nothing would be found at all. There was no other theory or any other type of investigation to pursue. It was simply a missing person case.

Tuesday brought rain, which grounded the helicopter and caused many searchers to give up. By Wednesday, most of the searchers had moved on, and only family, friends, and I continued to search. I had no doubt she had passed on by now, but I needed to find the body so that her husband could put her to rest with a proper burial. On Thursday, sadly, the operations commander announced the failure in this file, and all searching was called off. Hope was gone. I felt so bad that I had failed Mrs. Burke and the old man. I took a much-needed day off, knowing that we had given it our best. I thought I would just have to wait for the day that some hunter or hiker accidentally stumbled upon her skeletal remains so that we could finally put closure to the event, but this was not to be.

I started back to work on the Saturday night shift. I began the shift by visiting Mr. Burke to ask him how he was doing.

It had been a hard week for him. I told him to call me if he needed anything. I would help as best I could. He thanked me, and yes, he cried some more for his Mrs. Burke. It was a long Saturday night, now seven days since Mrs. Burke had disappeared.

On Sunday night, I was back on shift again. It was an exceptionally quiet night, and several hours into my shift, around three in the morning, I received a call from Dispatch.

"Five Alpha One. Dispatch."

I replied, "Five here. Go ahead, Dispatch."

"Ten-four. We just received a call of a prowler at a residence on Tower Road."

I turned the police car around and headed for Tower Road as I replied to Dispatch, "Go ahead with the details."

Dispatch explained, " A homeowner stated he was scared. He thought he heard a prowler in the bushes near his home. He was fearing a home invasion attack and asked for police to attend. He gave no other details. We have no suspect description."

"Ten-four, Dispatch. I am en route."

I rushed to the scene and radioed my arrival. "Dispatch, you can mark me ten-seven scene."

I then turned on the vehicle floodlights and blazed the property perimeter. The search turned up nothing. I could see the homeowner peeking through the window. I exited the police car, and he came to the door of his residence. I assured the homeowner it was probably a raccoon or perhaps even a bear not quite gone into hibernation. He accepted that explanation, and I moved on.

As I backed out of the driveway, I thought I saw some movement behind some trees near his property line. I took a closer look, and standing in the bush was a woman in rags. The rags were the remains of the dress belonging to Mrs. Burke. The dress was barely clinging to her frail body. Her skin was torn and scratched from her knees to her ankles. Her legs were plastered with dried, scabbed blood mixed with fresh, open wounds. It was all the result of walking through so many shrubs and thorns. I rushed to her aid, and I will never forget her words.

"Well, it's about time you found me!"

I found her about five kilometres from where she had disappeared. Shortly after, an ambulance took her off to the hospital (against her will—she just wanted to go home and have some tea!). At the hospital, the doctor determined that she would be fine. Her wounds were cleaned and dressed, and she was permitted to go home.

She had gone outside to go berry picking on her property, she got disoriented, walked in the wrong direction, and kept walking. For eight days! I am sure she did not walk alone. She lived to be ninety years old, and died warm and comfortable in her bed.

I was in a standoff and alone. Many emotions rippled through me as I listened to the cries of this man begging to be killed. The thoughts that flowed through my mind as time seemed to stand still were amazing. I wondered if my former colleagues and great friends, Ed and Harry, had felt this way during their standoff experiences. It was now my turn. Would mine end as tragically as theirs? I prayed that this would end soon—and peacefully.

— Chapter 14 —

So Easy to Die

Once upon a time, in a land far, far away, where the mountains were really large and the trees grew very, very tall . . .

So many years ago, at bedtime, our children's nightly routine often brought with it a bedtime story that I had composed. Each and every story commenced with that opening line. I spent countless hours storytelling, and I even fell asleep before some stories were finished. The stories were never the same. They were filled with excitement, adventure, and thrills, the kind of stories that children love to hear, and just like the opening line, the closing was also always the same. "And they lived happily ever after." The real world is not like that.

I had loaded my bright red Old Town Discovery canoe with food and supplies to last a week, and with Bill Rowe and his own loaded Mad River canoe, we set out onto the frigid waters of Takla Lake, in northern British Columbia. It was in November of 1989, and little did I know that this was the start of a journey that would forever haunt me. The journey took us south down the Takla Lake and into the Middle River. A lazy float down the Middle River brought us into the vast, frigid waters of Trembleur Lake. We sat on the shore of this lake for two days, waiting for the wind to subside before we could traverse it. Finally the wind died and we were able to cross. Once across, we hit the Grand Rapids at the mouth of the Tachie River. We floated through carefully, then proceeded down the long, winding Tachie River itself. Our journey ended at the small community of Tachie, on the northeast corner of Stuart Lake. I had no idea that a stop at this small community would begin a journey that has yet to end.

A few days earlier, while following this route, we had stopped at a small, isolated post called Leo Creek. An American fellow was living there, and because of the remoteness and isolation, I suspected he was running from something. During times of war, many Americans hid in this part of the country to avoid being drafted. I suspected this fellow might have been a draft dodger, but this certainly wasn't the time or place to quiz him, rather something to check out once I was back on duty. He had several chocolate Lab puppies that were several weeks old, and he asked if we would take a couple. I took one—I wasn't sure what to do with it, but it was so darn cute—Bill declined, and we were on our way. I knew I couldn't bring it home, because no pets were allowed in the place I was living at the time. I would figure something out. The puppy would find a home for sure.

We pulled up onto the shore of the community of Tachie, where we were to catch our ride back to town. Right away, a young fellow came running down to the shore to check us out. He was short, stocky, about sixteen years old, and very dark from the past summer's sun. He was extremely friendly and offered to help us unload our gear. I asked him his name, and he replied, "Ben."

He showed great interest in Trip—the perfect name I had christened the puppy with when I was crossing Trembleur Lake. Once all our gear was loaded and before driving off, I offered the puppy to Ben, and he ecstatically accepted. Bill and I drove off. My journey with Ben had just begun.

While posted to this small town, Tachie was part of my patrol area. As such, I would drive there once or twice a month to check things out—you know, just fly the flag, as we called it. Occasionally I would run into Ben, and I got to know him a little. He always thanked me again for Trip, who grew into quite a large Labrador retriever. Ben was always there to lend a hand whenever I was working in his community, but that was all about to change.

More than a year later, in January of 1991, in the cold, dead dark of winter, around two in the morning, I was in a deep slumber at home and was awakened by the ringing of my phone. The Telecoms operator explained to me that Matt and Harry were on duty and had received a call from a resident in the community of Tachie reporting that Ben was drunk and had held his girlfriend against her will. When she escaped, Ben shot her with a rifle. The shot struck her in the shoulder. She was freaking out, screaming and bleeding, and an ambulance had been called to assist her. Upon receiving all the details from Dispatch, Matt and Harry had proceeded to the scene. Telecoms were now calling me to attend the office, in case backup was needed. I thought this was an advantage, as I knew Ben. I would be able to call him and de-escalate this whole thing. I dressed and made it to the office in record time.

Once Harry and Matt arrived near Tachie, they had stopped several hundred feet short of the community to devise a plan. They were alone and didn't have the luxury of the RCMP's Emergency Response and Tactics (ERT) team. The ERT was a team of regular members who had been highly trained in combat techniques, specialized weapons training, and conflict resolution in the most complex of active person crimes. The problem was, they were for the most part located in larger centres, and it often took them hours to muster and attend such scenes as this. Time was not a luxury afforded to anyone in this event.

Being alone, Matt and Harry decided to enter the property through the bush in the back and contain the residence from two points. Then they would await my phone call to Ben. From the office, I would then make a phone call to Ben and convince him to come out to the waiting policemen. There should be no problem; we could do this. I made the call, and a drunken and barely coherent Ben answered the phone. I told him who I was, but he didn't understand. I told him I was the one who gave him Trip, but he still didn't recognize me, although he did add, "That dog was stupid. I killed that stupid thing!"

I was surprised to hear this, but I wasn't sure if it was true. One never can guess the accuracy of a statement coming from someone under the influence of alcohol or drugs. Either way, this was not going well. Ben slammed down the phone, and I heard a sharp *thunk* as the phone hit the floor. I radioed Matt and Harry and informed them of the failed attempt. Then I advised them I would be attending the scene to assist them. I ran from the office, fired up the old Suburban, and with lights flashing, I headed north to Tachie. While I was en route, a twenty-minute drive that seemed to take an hour, Matt and Harry would secure the house. While awaiting my arrival, whereupon we would devise another plan, Harry and Matt kept watch on the house. Harry was at the south side of the house and Matt at the north, so they couldn't see each other.

After some time had passed, and before my arrival, Matt heard Harry screaming, "Drop the gun!" Then, without a pause, there were two shots fired in rapid succession. Matt thought Harry had been shot, and his next thought was, *Shit. Where's Frank?*

I was still driving. Matt ran around the corner, and on the ground, near the steps to the house, Ben lay on his back. Matt explained that Harry was standing fifty feet away, white, pale, frozen, and speechless.

I rolled in a few minutes later, and on this frigid, moonlit night, my eyes locked onto Ben. He was wearing nothing but a pair of trousers and a dirty faded white T-shirt. He was missing a chunk of his left elbow from the one gunshot, and the second shot had created a small bloodstain in the centre of his chest. The redness of the blood was brilliant against the light coat of white snow that had fallen. I went over to where Ben lay, and I asked him if he was okay. There was no response. I'd never thought about it before this, but I guessed it made sense that you couldn't talk if there was a hole in your lungs. Air needs to pass over your vocal cords, or they won't work. Ben lay there, and he appeared to be talking, very briefly, without any sound, but only for an instant—and then he was gone. The first aid and CPR rendered could do nothing for him. Ben had died almost instantly. I still awake at times and see him lying there. That is an image that will stay with me forever.

The coroner's inquest determined that before I had a chance to arrive at the scene and call Ben out of the house, Ben had spotted Harry. He burst out the front door with his rifle poised to shoot. Harry justifiably fired in self-defence and was never charged. I can't imagine what pain he must have suffered following that standoff. Harry was never one to talk much.

Matt was also affected by this event. He remained quiet for a long time following that standoff and just seemed to stare off into space. He would eventually come around, but no doubt he still carries horrible images of that event with him to this day. The young girlfriend made a full recovery. As for me, many nights over the years I have awakened from horrible dreams, sweating. I know that if Ben had seen me first, he would not have died at eighteen. He never finished his last words, and I always wondered what those words might have been. I could only hope he was saying, "I didn't mean to hurt anyone."

I never saw Trip again.

After that, I always feared being in the situation that Harry was thrown into. I feared that I wouldn't be able to handle it. I feared that I might screw up. I always wished that I would one day retire and be able to brag that in thirty-two years I had never hurt anyone. I had thought that one day there would be a chance that I would be involved in a bank holdup, face to face with some moron armed with a gun or a knife. I always got scared wondering how I would handle it. I never saw this one coming. Then, there I was. I didn't want to be there. I just wanted to go home.

My former co-worker and great friend Ed was also in a similar situation.

— Chapter 15 —

Saving Christmas

All men are afraid of battle. The coward is the one who lets his fear overcome his sense of duty. Duty is the essence of a police officer.

In my early years of service, while stationed in northern BC, my wife, Diane, our children, and I were posted to a detachment with some amazingly wonderful people. Among them were Ed and Jen. Ed and I worked together and became close friends. Our first big file together, which cemented our closeness, happened when we attended a murder scene where an eighteen-year-old male had blasted his uncle's head off with a shotgun. Unbelievably, his motive was an unpaid bill at the local pool hall. We spent hours together working on this file, gathering evidence and producing a solid case that led to the conviction of the accused.

The closeness at work spilled over into our personal lives and those of our children. It helped that the children were all of the same age. We were constantly back and forth to each other's homes and socialized often. It was a special friendship, such that if we got together next year, or in ten years, we could pick up exactly where we left off, as if no time had elapsed since we had last been together.

In this job, there was always a bond with other police officers, but some bonds were more special than others. The bond with Ed was that way. Sometimes you may work together with the same person for a few months, or occasionally as long as five years. Sadly, all partnerships in this job had the same ending. Transfers to new locations were assigned, and everyone moved on.

Finally, that day came, and it was our turn to move on, Ed to the west, and I to central British Columbia. Ed decided to take on the job as the detachment commander. He was going to be the man in charge, the big cheese.

Early in my career I had developed a little routine. It became an annual habit that I religiously executed every Christmas Eve. I made a point, whether I was working or off for Christmas, to call Telecoms and wish the working staff all the best of the festive season. Telecoms were often forgotten. They were our lifeline, and they were great at what they did. They put up with nonsense and verbal abuse from some callers that most people can't even begin to imagine. They are a little-known core of dedicated workers who save lives, behind the scenes. Without them, patrol officers would be dead in the water. I just felt that a Christmas wish at this time of year was my little way of saying thank you, showing an appreciation for what they did.

So, around 11:00 p.m. on Christmas eve in 1993, I made the annual call to our dispatch centre, which was located in the city. That particular dispatch centre was responsible for about four detachments in that region. Upon wishing them the best of the season, the distraught operator at the other end replied, "Oh, it's not a very merry Christmas at all."

I asked why, and the operator replied that there was a big domestic dispute in the detachment area where Ed was stationed. The domestic dispute had turned violent, with the husband attacking his wife, causing her to suffer life-threatening injuries. The husband was extremely intoxicated and had smashed her in the head with a beer bottle. A neighbour heard the commotion and had called the police. When the husband heard the police car siren, he escaped in his vehicle and was pursued by one of our members for about forty-five minutes before coming to a dead-end road. The member was cornered, and the violent husband charged at him with a rifle. Our member was forced to kill him.

Things were not good.

The operator was busy, so I ended the call and wished her the best. I remember going to bed on Christmas Eve thinking how lucky Ed was. I knew that, because he was in charge, he got to spend Christmas Eve with his family. I also knew he would be busy the next day.

After a coffee or two on Christmas morning, I called down to Ed and Jen's home to wish them a merry Christmas and to poke a little fun at Ed because he was stuck working Christmas Day. Jen didn't seem all that excited that I had called, but she did say that Ed was at the office. Then I started chuckling. "Ha, ha, he has to work."

And Jen replied, "No Frank, it was Ed."

Stupidly, I said, "Yeah, I know. It sucks that he has to work because of this shooting. How is the member doing who shot the guy, anyway?"

In a soft, scared voice, Jen replied, "Frank, it was Ed. It was Ed, Frank."

It finally hit me.

I had put my foot in my mouth with enough force to almost choke on it. It hit me hard. I apologized to Jen profusely and offered some comforting words. It didn't seem to matter.

What the hell was Ed doing working Christmas Eve? Bosses didn't work Christmas Eve, I thought.

Jen explained briefly what had happened. I would learn later how it had unfolded.

When the domestic complaint came in, Ed went to the office to lend a hand. That was just the kind of guy that Ed was. Ed knew the area where the suspect had gone, so he set out to capture him. There had been no information received that the suspect had a firearm or access to a firearm, so with confidence, Ed sent the other officers home to be with their families, and he set out alone.

Several minutes into Ed's travel, he spotted the suspect's vehicle and followed it. It was a long, winding, abandoned logging road that ended in a cul de sac configuration. When they came to the end of the road, the suspect jumped out of his vehicle with the rifle and charged toward Ed. The suspect then raised the rifle, with a gesture that signified he intended to shoot. Ed didn't have time to open his own door to get out, nor did he have time to roll down his window. Ed shot first through the windshield, then the driver's side window as the suspect came closer. Ed watched the suspect collapse. The wounds were fatal. The spray of glass had cut Ed's face and hands in several places. In the sudden explosiveness of the encounter, Ed thought he had also been hit and believed that he would bleed to death. It took the attending paramedics some time to assure him that he would be okay.

I apologized to Jen. She said she was okay with it, but she was worried about Ed. We exchanged a few more subdued greetings, and I hung up the phone. It was around eleven in the morning, and my wife, Diane, was just putting together the stuffing for the Christmas turkey. She knew by the concerned look on my face that something was wrong. I said, "It was Ed who was involved in that shooting. He killed the guy."

Diane's face went blank. There was nothing she could say.

I then said, "Let's pack everything up. We are going to Ed and Jen's."

Diane didn't argue, didn't hesitate, didn't plan. We just loaded our things, including the turkey with all the trimmings. The children packed up their prized possessions from Santa, and we were off. All of our own Christmas traditions and plans for the few days ahead had changed, just like that, and we were unfazed. It was just one of those things that had to be done. It happens sometimes.

Three hours later, after travelling over snow-covered mountain roads, we pulled into Ed and Jen's driveway. Jen answered the door. Through tears, she cried, "You saved our Christmas!"

We all embraced each other and shared warm hugs.

After unloading the turkey and luggage, it was time for me to go see Ed. I wasn't sure how he was, or how he would react. After all, he had just killed a man. I drove slowly to the office. Upon entering, I noticed several officers from the city headquarters had come there to console Ed and investigate, despite the fact it was Christmas Day. These policemen had put their own plans on hold and left their families behind to come here to deal with this crisis.

The event itself would require an impeccable investigation. As for Ed, he was a wreck. The attending members had no idea what to do with him, and they were afraid for his well-being. A member greeted me at the door and asked who I was, and I told him I was a member and Ed's friend. I told him I knew what had happened, and I explained that my wife and I felt Ed and Jen could use some familiar faces. I said, "We have come to spend Christmas with them."

We still weren't sure how Ed would react. In my experience, I wouldn't have been surprised if, in his stressed frame of mind, he would tell me to screw off.

The member said, "I'll go get Ed."

He disappeared into a back office, and just seconds later, Ed appeared around the corner. As he realized it was me, a small smile broke free on his distressed face. "Am I ever glad to see you!"

He grabbed me, and his giant hug soon turned into tears of

relief as I said, "Let's go home. We have families waiting for us. I'll build you a big rum!"

One of the city boys shook my hand profusely. "Thank you," he cried. "We can all go home to our families because of you."

Our families were excited when I returned with Ed so quickly. We begin a feast of food and drinks like I had never seen before. The contribution of our turkey, thrown in with Jen's ham, proved more than enough food for all. Ed never mentioned the standoff once. We sat around the fireplace and told stories of better days gone by. It was 3:00 a.m. before Ed finally passed out. I'm not sure if it was from total exhaustion—or the rum.

Ed had no time at all, and so far, I was still standing. Cold, tired, and scared, but I was still standing. Now with my pistol locked between Burt's eyes, I was in control. He knew it, too. I was alone, but in control. Then, in the background, I heard a vehicle. I heard it screeching to a stop, and then the doors opened. Three minutes, five minutes, eight minutes had passed—I was not sure. But it didn't matter anymore. I was in control, and my backup had arrived. Just seconds later, Adam was on my right, Calvin on my left, and both now locked onto the target. Burt's odds had just changed dramatically.

He will drop the machete, I thought. *Any sane man would.*

But no, he was not sane. He thrust the machete toward Calvin and then started yelling, louder than before, "Come on, shoot me, you must have more guts than that pig cop there!"

It seemed like a new energy had come over him now. With three pistols aimed at him, he would surely get his wish. However, Calvin did not fire. Adam did not fire. Burt's screams were met with silence. Then I calmly spoke.

"Burt, put down the knife. We can help you."

By this time his look of frustration had grown into one of fury. He wanted to die. We didn't want to engage, but we would shoot to kill if we had to. He took a step backward. When I saw this, I figured that with three of us on him now, he was overwhelmed. We were in his space. A step backward gave him back this space, his comfort zone. Then he took another step back. It struck me—he was backing up, he wanted to get inside the house. We were not answering his plea to shoot him, so he was going to escalate this by running inside and grabbing who knows what. It hit me then. I realized his girlfriend was inside. I had forgotten about his girlfriend.

The original complaint was that he was holding his girlfriend hostage inside. Where the hell was she? The driveway encounter had been going on for what seemed like a long time, so why had she not left the house? I thought that maybe she had slipped out through some other door. Then I thought, *Is she dead? Cut down by the machete?* Maybe by some miracle she had survived. I felt she was already gone. It only made sense; otherwise, she would have run out.

I didn't see any blood. The machete's edge was clean.

Burt continued to back up, moving closer to the entrance door. He wanted to go back inside. Why? Would he come out with the machete to her throat? Would he come out with a shotgun, a rifle, or a pistol? Would he even come out at all? A thousand thoughts ran through my head. The light breeze felt even colder then. He was not far from the door, and he was still backing toward it, ever so slowly. He was not yelling now. I edged forward, as I felt he was getting too far away. Calvin and Adam followed. We closed the gap. We were now in control. We could not let him get inside. If he got inside, the game would change, and he would surely win, if there was to be a winner.

I commanded him again, "Burt, don't move any farther. Put down the knife. Let's talk about this. Goddamn it, put down the knife!"

"Fuck you, asshole."

He was too close to the door. Close enough now that my stomach wrenched again. He could not go inside. I could only hope that Calvin and Adam were thinking the same. We moved closer, with pistols still trained on him. He was backing slowly, still holding the machete high, ready to strike. I was thinking of ways to get to him without getting struck. He was now a couple of feet from the door.

My thoughts raced. So many thoughts. He was too close. I had failed. We had failed.

The threat cue was there. He had charged me, and I did not fire. This could have ended, and I would have been justified in killing him. All I could think now was that it would get much worse. Then more panic. Notes. Facts. Records. All would be needed, and up to that point I had nothing. I didn't even know what time it was anymore or how long I had stood here. Now he wanted to get inside.

It had been beaten into us, a basic survival rule of police work, pounded into us during training over and over again: *He was not to go inside!* Yet it now appeared he would get inside and kill his girlfriend, if he hadn't already. He would probably come charging out, blasting whatever weapon he had secretly hidden in there. I made the decision.

I must shoot. I can't let him go inside.

Then I hesitated. I could not shoot now. I would surely be damned for not having shot him yet, taking him out when I should have. Why was he now backing up? The critics would say he was surrendering, going inside to get a jacket to warm himself. *I'm going to lose this. I must kill this man.* I was confused. What could I do? I had to clear my head and think.

— Chapter 16 —

A Questionable Decision

It has been said that there is no time like the present. But in fact, there is no present like time.

I couldn't let him go inside. If he did, this could turn very ugly very fast. Enough was enough. I had waited for what seemed like an eternity. I had given him ample opportunity to lay down the machete. Hell, I had even offered him help with his issues. It was freezing cold now, and I was shivering uncontrollably. Whether it was from the cold wind or the adrenalin rush, I didn't know. I was exhausted. Burt was not giving up. He wanted to get inside. My stomach burned, and my head hurt. Calvin and Adam had not fired. I had no idea what they were thinking. This had been my show from the start, so maybe they were waiting for me to make a decision. Yes, that had to be it. I had to decide. Burt had begged me to shoot him. He waved the machete. I felt I would be justified. He took one more step backwards. He was now within an arm's reach of the door. I was then totally certain of my decision. It had been long enough. I was focused directly onto his head, and I slowly began to squeeze the cold metal trigger.

Then I stopped. I couldn't shoot him now.

In the twenty years before this incident, I had seen the repercussions of suspects being shot and killed by police, and it was not pretty. I hadn't killed anyone before, and I couldn't begin to imagine the stresses that other police officers had gone through. Burt was not in the house yet—there was still time. If I shot now, this is how this event would unfold:

The shot would be loud, and ring out like thunder exploding in my head. It would be a perfect hit. I would see an explosion of blood and fragmented tissue erupting from just below his right eye. Both of his arms would collapse. The machete would fall in what appeared to be slow motion toward the ground. Burt would buckle at the knees, and then fall backwards. He would hit the gravel with a sickly thump. He would not move. He would not cry. He would not yell out for help.

Nothing.

He would not breathe.

He would be gone.

If I fired the shot, the rest of the story wouldn't get any better. This is how it would be written: justifiably, I thought, I had killed a man. Calvin and Adam would check him. He'd be gone. Yes, he'd be dead. I'd be alone. Calvin would not speak. Adam would not speak. I would not speak. They would not look at me. From there, everything would be a blur.

I'd see him lifeless. It would be like looking through a thick fog. People would be speaking, but I would not hear anything.

A lifetime of thoughts and dreams would now all be gone. It would feel like my heart and soul and every fibre of my existence was spiralling down into a deep crevice. The whole event would seem surreal. I would not believe that I had killed a man. My life would be forever changed.

Before long, I'd just sit at home, suspended from my job, awaiting the outcome of the investigation. Statements, then more statements, and media bombardment, all combined with harassment by police, and then the coroner's inquest would follow. Days would turn into months, and the process would drag on for years. Post-traumatic stress disorder would set in. Then there would be prescription drugs to combat the depression. The critics all scream that if I'd felt threatened, why didn't I shoot as soon as Burt initially charged me with the machete? Why this? Why that? In coffee shops and hallways, from Victoria to St. John's, everyone would have an opinion. Some would think I should have fired, yet others would think I was wrong. Many hope I go to jail. Everyone out there has their own expert opinion. Neighbours now look the other way when they see me. Strangers drive by to see where I live. As they pass by, they say to each other, "That's it, right there, that's where he lives." Some would even ask, "Why didn't he shoot the machete out of his hand?" They've seen that in movies.

The event would be in the headlines everywhere, ranging from "He was justified," to "He murdered him in cold blood." Then my son innocently asks, "Dad, did you really kill a man?"

I can only answer with tears as I hug him for some comfort. There is no way he could understand, but he hugs me back, anyway.

Then, finally, that dreaded day arrives. The investigation is now complete, resulting in breaking news!

"Mountie Charged With First-Degree Murder."

I sit at home, very sick and alone. Alcohol becomes my friend. I watch hours of television but never see a thing. I know that soon I will be dragged through the courts. My job is gone while I await the results of the trial. I was told one time that it was better to be judged by twelve than carried by six. But at that time I didn't feel it was true.

Weight falls from my frail frame. I am but a ghost of the man I once was, and I am very sick.

The organization that I once worshipped is now seeking to make an example of me. How did this come to be? I was prepared to die for them, and now I am their most wanted. I was cast into a standoff and made a decision. It was justified, I thought, taking into consideration the provisions of Canada's Criminal Code. I felt I had shown incredible restraint, and I had made no panicked decisions. It was he, not I, who wanted to die. But now, I felt more dead than him.

The Criminal Code says that if I feared grievous bodily harm, I could use as much force as is necessary to prevent this harm. Months before, on the day of the standoff, there was no lawyer present, no prosecutor was there, and no judge was there. There were not twelve jury members present. Nobody, just Burt and me. But now, all of these people have to decide whether or not I feared grievous bodily harm. They didn't feel the panic, the shivering, or how frightened I had been, wondering if I was going home to my family that night. They didn't feel my stomach burn or the fear that I felt when I was thinking what I should do if he charged me. They didn't feel how scared I was or how alone I felt, even when my backup arrived.

They felt nothing. They knew nothing.

Yet now, with all their wisdom, intelligence, and training, they would decide whether or not I had feared grievous bodily harm and if I was justified in shooting this sick man.

So, if I had killed him, no greater hell awaited. There had to be another way. Unlike so many other police officers who have been attacked with weapons, I had been given time. I didn't know why his initial charge had halted. Maybe it was the sudden precision with which I had engaged him, or maybe he saw me as a familiar face from his past. I didn't know. I would never know. What I did know was that he was not going back inside.

— Chapter 17 —

The Takedown

I am a police officer. I did not write the law. I may even disagree with some laws, but I will enforce them. Behind this badge is a heart just like yours. I bleed. I think. I love. I cry, and, yes, I can be killed. Although I am but one man, I have thousands of brothers and sisters who would die for me, as I would for them. If you take on me, you have taken on all of us.

I could not let him get inside.

I was in control.

He was now ready to open the door, and when he reached for the knob, it was stuck. His guard was down, momentarily. Without thinking, he lowered the machete as he turned slightly to pull on the doorknob. The door opened, and he turned away to slip inside. In that great moment of opportunity, offered seemingly from the gods, Adam charged him from behind, closing the twenty-foot gap in milliseconds. Without a conscious decision to do so, I followed. The weight of both of us drove Burt forward into the opposite wall, smashing the drywall and cracking a wooden wall stud. The force knocked the machete from his hand, but it landed within easy reach. Before he could grab it again, I stepped on it, pinning it to the floor.

Instinctively, we grabbed Burt by the neck and head and pulled him backwards, out through the open door. He grabbed the inside frame. I slammed his arm with my fist, breaking it free. Adam slammed his other hand, which quickly released. Adam had his arm around Burt's neck and pulled hard, causing Burt to come backwards out the door, stumbling and falling. I stumbled, also falling backwards, as Burt crashed onto me. Adam was still hanging on to his neck. The small confines of the porch prevented Calvin from jumping in, but now that he was outside, Calvin began slamming him with a three-foot-long metal baton. This hulk of a man began to stand, with Calvin smashing him on the back and ribs. Adam was trying to choke the life out of him, and now I slipped from underneath him and began pounding his ribs with my fists. Slowly, we got him back to the ground. He fought on. His beastly metabolic strength, spurred on by the alcohol and possibly a quantity of unknown drugs, meant this man would fight to the end. Then I remembered my pepper spray. I reached down to my duty belt, and first felt my pistol. When I charged Burt, I must have locked it back into its holster, even though I had no memory of doing so. I slid my hand along the belt, grabbing on to the pepper spray, and pulling it from its pouch. I flipped open the safety catch and depressed the button. At point-blank range, I unloaded a blast directly into his eyes. He gasped and choked. He went limp and began gasping for air.

I felt him change. He had no less strength, but instead of fighting, he was diverting his efforts to deal with his burning eyes. He screamed, "Jesus Christ, I can't breathe, I can't see!"

The spray had left him gasping for breath. Tears fell from his eyes. Mucus streamed from his nose.

I grabbed my handcuffs and torqued his left hand behind his back, and with a snap I had secured one cuff. Adam swung the second arm back, and I heard the click of the locking mechanism. It was the sweet sound of conquest. Success. Victory. We had won. I had won. No one died that day. We would all be able to go home.

Burt had nothing left. It took all three of us to lift him, body and bones, into the back seat of the police car. He lay stretched out on the bench from door to door.

He was still gasping and yelling, "I can't breathe, I can't breathe!"

Adam said, "Frank, he can't breathe."

I remembered back to the time of Ben's death, following his encounter with Harry. I remembered how Ben tried to talk but couldn't because of a hole in his chest. I said, "Adam, think about it, man. If he can talk, he can breathe." I then asked Adam to watch over Burt, as it was now time to collect the machete and focus my attention on Burt's girlfriend. I first picked up the machete and noticed for the first time how harmless it was. The handle was still warm from Burt's grasp as I secured it in the trunk of the police car.

Next, Burt's girlfriend. I cautiously entered the house through the same door we had just smashed through. I was hit with an overwhelming stench of urine-soaked laundry. The place was filthy. The kitchen counter was strewn with unwashed dishes, and a layer of hardened white grease filled a portion of a frying pan that sat on a stained and food-encrusted stovetop. Nothing appeared to have been washed for days. I walked around the corner from the kitchen into the living room and found Burt's girlfriend.

She was lying stretched out on the couch, wrapped in a stained blanket. I wondered if she was alive. There was no movement that I could see. I approached slowly, thinking I was about to find a corpse, but then I saw that she was breathing. There were no visible injuries to her face. I nudged her gently. She stirred and then woke up. She looked at me, dazed and confused, and then asked in slurred speech, "Where am I?"

Her breath had a foul stench of liquor, and it was obvious that she was totally intoxicated. The paramedics, who had arrived a few minutes earlier, were able to check her over. She was fine. Burt had not harmed her at all. He'd only said that he'd hurt her just to provoke us into killing him. She knew nothing of the standoff and had slept through the whole thing. Or, more accurately, she had been unconscious throughout the whole event.

Calvin asked, "Is she okay?"

"She's fine," I replied.

Calvin said he would deal with her as I returned to my police car to assist Adam. Upon reaching my car, I asked Adam how Burt was doing. Adam, being a fast learner, replied, "Well, he is still complaining, so I guess he is still breathing!" I chuckled as Adam walked to his own car. Turning to look back at me, he shouted, "I'll meet you at the prisoner bay for the next round!"

— Chapter 18 —

You Have Got to Be Kidding Me

To succeed in life, you must always expect the best, plan for the worst, and be prepared for all surprises.

I reversed the patrol car out of Burt's driveway, turning onto the street. Still out of breath, I radioed dispatch.

"Dispatch, Five Alpha One."

"Go ahead, Five Alpha One."

"I'm ten-eight, RTO with one adult male in custody." RTO is police lingo for "returning to office."

"Ten-four," Dispatch replied. "We'll advise the guardroom."

The return drive to the office was comforting. Burt was in custody, he was cuffed, and amazingly, he was still breathing. He lay stretched across the back seat, snorting and sniffling from the burn of the pepper spray. As I relaxed, for the first time, I noticed that the back of my left hand was swollen and bruised. Only now, it had started to hurt. I adjusted my seating as I drove, and I also noticed that a pain was arching through my lower back. Battle wounds, I thought.

A short time later, I arrived with Burt in tow at the detachment prisoners' area. The large steel bay doors slowly rolled up. I drove inside, and the doors rolled down behind me. Adam and Calvin arrived shortly after, entering through a side door in the prisoner bay. We all then approached the back door of the patrol car to remove our prisoner. I opened the door expecting a new battle, but there was none. Burt was lying limp on the seat and still gasping from the pepper spray. Adam grasped one foot, Calvin the other, and we pulled Burt out as far as his waist. We then pulled him backwards by his shoulders and raised him to his feet.

He was crying profusely, and mucus streamed from his burning sinuses. He begged for relief from the pepper spray.

Without a fight, we escorted him down the long corridor to an eye-flush station near one of the prisoner cells. Once there, he flushed gallons of water into his swollen, bloodshot eyes, which provided a relief to him as the water diluted the pepper spray. He began to relax.

After Burt's Charter Rights were explained to him, he asked for a lawyer. Adam promptly got on the phone and made the call to alert Burt's lawyer. His lawyer didn't ask to speak to Burt, but instead stated that he would head directly to the office.

While awaiting the arrival of his lawyer, Burt needed to

be thoroughly searched and lodged in a jail cell. He had settled down. There was no fight left. The handcuffs were removed, and he was searched.

His shirt was lifted for a thorough visual search. Then came a surprise. Adam, Calvin, and I looked at each other in disbelief. His back and ribs were criss-crossed with black and blue contusions. It was as if he had been nailed to the ground, then kicked repeatedly with steel-toed boots.

I first wondered if this had been done beforehand. Had he been in an accident before our encounter? Maybe he was one of those people with that weird disease that causes a person to bruise easily. My mind was racing. Had Calvin smacked him that many times with the metal baton? Maybe I had punched much harder than I had thought. I couldn't be sure. I did know that, no matter what the cause, we had arrested him, and we had used force to do so. His injuries could now support a claim that the force was excessive.

Burt had no fight left and was now compliant. He was placed in the jail cell without further incident.

Burt's lawyer was on his way, and I was certain that when he saw Burt's injuries, he would surely cry excessive force. Once again, my stomach was churning, because this guy had put me through hell and could now possibly walk freely from court proceedings. The evidence surely showed that more force was used to arrest him than was necessary. The fact that Burt had charged me with a machete would probably be forgotten. His Charter Rights had been violated. I felt even sicker than before.

A short while later, Burt's lawyer arrived at the office. He asked to meet with Burt privately. Burt was removed from the jail cell and taken to a private room with the lawyer.

All the restraint that I had shown, the plea for Burt to drop the machete, and my decision not to shoot, were all now meaningless. Burt had begged to die, and now that meant nothing. His lawyer would no doubt claim he was subjected to excessive force, and I might even be charged with assault. I wondered where this would go.

After several minutes, as predicted, the lawyer emerged from the interview room and said, "Get me a camera." My guts rolled.

"This is insane," I whispered.

It was a long wait while the lawyer had his time with Burt—time for me to write some notes and complete the booking paper. Eventually the lawyer came out and Burt was secured back into the cell. I then removed the machete from the police car, labelled and tagged it, and secured it in the exhibit locker. I then proceeded to the hospital to seek treatment for my throbbing hand. I was not sure which hurt more, my back or my stomach. But my head was worse.

The hospital wait was very short. The attending physician ordered X-rays following his brief but thorough exam, so off to X-ray I went. Following the examination, there was a brief wait. Soon, the doctor stepped into the office to tell me that there was a contusion to the back of the hand, which had caused a bone bruise. It would heal. Unfortunately, the news about my back injury was not so encouraging.

"There appears to be disc damage," he said.

After his diagnosis, he referred me to a specialist.

That's just great, I thought, as I left his office.

I boarded my police car and headed back to my detachment office. An eerie calm had settled over me. I arrived shortly after and took comfort from the fact that Burt's lawyer had long since departed. Burt was fast asleep in his cell. The paperwork began.

— Chapter 19 —

The Process

How strange humans are. Here sits a man who was fighting for his death. Now he sits fighting for his life.

Now that Burt was in custody, there were several options available in the judicial process relevant to his release. Police have the authority to release him with a document that is a promise to appear in court at a later date. They can also add conditions to his release or attempt a remand in custody. Given the circumstances of Burt's actions, the most logical option was to pursue a remand in custody. With a successful show-cause hearing, a remand into custody would be inevitable. A show-cause hearing is a brief meeting with a Justice of the Peace where the justifiable reasons are explained as to why a prisoner should not be released. If the hearing was successful, it would mean that Burt would stay in jail until his first court appearance. Following that first court appearance, the judge may order a further remand, or a release with or without conditions. There were numerous variables and factors to consider before the whole matter was resolved.

As predicted, Burt was remanded into custody to await trial. These would be long days for Burt. He would sit or lie in a cell that measured eight feet by eight feet, with four walls of cement and a cement floor. The entry and exit to this cold room was a large sliding steel door. The door had a small, wire-reinforced window and a lower sliding hatch. The hatch gave access to pass food and such back and forth in a secure way so as not to endanger the jail guard. Inside, a single steel bunk was bolted against the far wall. In one corner there was a stainless steel one-piece toilet with a small steel sink built into the top. A cold water faucet was moulded to the sink, and there was no hot water. There was no TV, no radio or music, and unlike the movies, there were no rats, either! If the guard in charge of watching over Burt was in a good mood, he might turn up the volume on his personal radio so that Burt could listen in. Burt might even be treated to a magazine or a book. Other than that, in these situations, time drags very slowly. Days are very long, and nights are even longer. This room was referred to as "a suite in the Queen's palace."

Burt was charged with several serious Criminal Code offences. Given his violent nature, the attack, and his past history, a release with conditions was not an option. Surprisingly, his lawyer did not dispute this. He had another plan. His plan was to start with a not guilty plea. Then he would attempt to convince the court that his client was beaten so badly that his

Charter Rights were violated. If it was determined that his rights had been violated, Burt would surely be acquitted. Considering the photos of the bruises and the beating to Burt's torso, his lawyer would surely prevail.

I lay awake many nights before the trial in anticipation of what might happen. I had a sick feeling that Burt would walk, which in police lingo means a person was not convicted of a crime. Those few moments in the standoff submerged me into a hell that lasted for weeks. Maybe I would get lucky for once and his lawyer would not ask that an investigation be launched against us for excessive force against his client. Yeah, right, like that was going to happen! Regardless, I would surely face a suspension from my own organization while they conducted their own investigation into whether or not excessive force had been used. Yes, Burt's days were long, but mine were even longer.

— Chapter 20 —

Justice on Trial

If you tell only the truth, it will become part of your past. If you tell only lies, it will become part of your future.

Awaiting the trial date allowed me time to prepare. I had to give the required evidence and somehow convince the court that the beating Burt had suffered was justified. Was there some way to present the evidence in a manner such that everything was revealed, yet the brutality of the beating was not exposed? I had been in the organization long enough to know that this might not end well. Burt's lawyer would present the photos, and I might have to accept the fact that Burt would walk. The troublesome part of it all was what might happen to me.

As I looked back over the years and recalled all that I had seen and done, I made a decision about that upcoming trial. It was the only decision that was right. It was the only thing that I knew. I decided that I would tell the truth—the honest, brutal truth. "Yes, Your Honour, I beat him, I beat him hard."

Finally, the big day arrived. I did not get much sleep the night before, a common trend in that line of work. I rolled out of bed. My hand had long since healed, but my back still hurt. The damage done during the arrest had progressed into degenerative disc disease. I just had to live with it. It would always hurt. I felt fortunate, though. It could have been much worse, as there were so many who lived with diseases and ailments that shortened their lives. I was awake far too early in anticipation of what that day would bring. To combat the lack of sleep, I had coffee, and then more coffee. I did not put bullets in my cornflakes that morning—my stomach was just a little off.

I showered, dressed, and made my way to the courthouse. It was a beautiful spring day with warm sunshine and a slight breeze. I had plenty of time before my court duty, so I grabbed another takeout coffee on the way. Shortly thereafter, I pulled into the courthouse parking lot. I still had plenty of time, so I finished my coffee. I went over the event in my head, rehearsing the story I was about to present. Over and over, I convinced myself that things would be all right, but then I also thought, *Yeah, right, who am I trying to kid?*

The wait was finally over, and it was time to go inside. It was almost 10:00 a.m. The court would be in session within minutes. Once I went inside the main doors, I headed to the corridor adjacent to the courtroom and took a seat in the hall. There were other people present for various reasons, and I didn't know any of them. The courtroom door opened, and the Crown attorney spoke.

"The Crown calls its first witness, Constable Frank Pitts."

The sheriff stepped outside the courtroom door, looked down the hall, and then reiterated the Crown's request.

"Constable Frank Pitts to the courtroom, please."

I stood up from my seat, collected myself, checked my uniform and grooming, and in stoic fashion, I walked into the courtroom. I gave a respectful bow to the court and stood silent in the aisle. The sheriff shut the door behind me.

I had done this many times before, but this time it came with a new fear. I had never been attacked with a machete, and I still didn't know if the actions I had taken were correct and justified. I thought it had been handled perfectly until I saw how badly Burt was bruised and beaten. The outcome scared me. I thought that Burt would walk and that I would get charged with assault.

The court clerk was seated directly in front of the judge. The judge's bench was on a dais, raised higher than the rest of the court area, separate from the clerk. The court clerk looked to me and asked, "Would you please take the stand?"

She pointed to a raised podium adjacent to the judge's bench. I approached the bench and performed a second respectful bow to the court. I then turned to the left and approached the witness box and stepped inside. I noticed there was no jury. Burt, in consultation with his lawyer, had chosen trial by judge alone. At the bench, facing the judge, was seated the defence lawyer. Burt was seated to the far right of the courtroom, inside the prisoner box. The Crown prosecutor sat to the far right, at the same table as the defence lawyer.

The court clerk spoke again. "Take the Bible into your right hand."

I picked up the Bible as ordered, and the court clerk then asked, "Do you intend to tell the truth, the whole truth, and nothing but the truth, so help you God?"

Cradling the Bible with both hands, I replied, "I do."

The court clerk continued. "State your name for the record, please."

I spoke calmly. "I am Constable Frank Paul Pitts. I am a regular member of the Royal Canadian Mounted Police and have been so for over twenty years. I am currently stationed in this community and was so stationed on November 3, 2002."

As was customary, traditional, and appropriate, the judge rarely looked up. He did not look at the accused, the defence, the Crown, or me. He just looked down and occasionally stared off into space. He wore his wire-rimmed glasses loosely, hanging on the end of his nose. He just wanted to hear the facts and to render his decision.

Burt was on trial for several serious Criminal Code offences. This was a massive turn of events, considering his original plan was for me to execute him. Instead of being at this trial, I could just as easily have been at a coroner's inquest explaining why I had chosen to kill him. Conversely, his original attack might have been fatal for me.

The trial began with the Crown and defence lawyers bantering, back and forth at each other, over some preliminary issues before the evidence in the trial was examined. Argument upon argument, it just seemed to go on forever. I was thinking, *Let's get this thing started.* I was anxious. My future lay in the balance.

The judge assertively interrupted the arguing, and without looking up, he stated, "You may be seated, Constable, if you wish."

I replied, "Thank you, Your Honour," but I remained standing. I had been told by my trainer a long time ago that, out of respect for the court, you do not sit. I'd wondered if this was some sort of test, presented by the judge to see what I would do. I have never taken a seat while on the stand.

The Crown attorney looked to me and asked, "Constable, were you on duty on November 3, 2002?"

I replied, "Yes, Your Honour, and I was in full working uniform." Witnesses address the bench, not the lawyers questioning them.

The Crown prosecutor then asked, "Did you have some sort of encounter that day?"

"Yes I did, Your Honour. I had an encounter with that gentleman seated right there wearing the blue shirt." I pointed to Burt.

The Crown looked toward the judge and stated, "For the record, Your Honour, the accused has been identified."

Then the Crown looked toward me. "Can you explain to the court what this encounter involved?"

I had dreaded it, had lost sleep about it, and had been sick about it. Finally, it was here. I began to talk, and the Crown listened intently. The defence prepared to interject at the first opportunity. I was allowed to speak, so I spoke honestly. I was ready to tell my story. I looked toward the judge. He continued to look down, scribbling and taking notes.

I started my story. I told it as I remembered it. I did not refer to notes. I spoke from my heart. "Your Honour," I said, as I respectfully addressed the court, "on November 3, 2002, I was in full working uniform and on duty working a scheduled day shift. I was busy attending a vehicle accident complaint when I got called to return to the office. So, I cleared from that complaint and drove my marked police car back to the office."

"What time was that, Constable?" asked the Crown.

I replied, "It was around lunchtime. Yes, approximately noon."

"Go on," the Crown directed.

I continued. "Once I got to the office, I was briefed by two other officers. I was told that Burt James had called the office and said that he was holding his girlfriend against her will at his home. He had stated to Dispatch that if anyone came to help her, he would kill them. He also said that it didn't matter who came, whether it was the police, paramedics, or whoever, he would kill them."

"Then what happened?"

"Well, myself and the other two officers proceeded to the scene to assess the situation. I drove the lead car, as I was familiar with the address. Once I got there, I pulled into the driveway and noticed my backup kept on driving past the street that I had turned onto. I wasn't sure what the other two officers were doing. So, I got out of the car, and was going to wait for them to return before we knocked on the door. But when I got out of the car, Burt came charging out of the house through the ground-level entry door with a machete in his right hand. I pulled out my revolver from my holster and targeted on him and yelled for him to stop. He was screaming like a madman. It scared the hell out of me."

The Crown stopped me and said, "You said you pulled out your revolver. Can you describe this for the court?"

I answered, "I'm sorry, Your Honour, it is not a revolver. It is a nine-millimetre semi-automatic handgun. I had said 'revolver' out of habit because, during my first ten or so years of service, we carried a revolver."

The Crown continued. "You said he was screaming. What was he screaming?"

I replied, "Well, he was yelling for me to kill him. He kept screaming at me, 'Shoot me, you fucking pig, shoot me.' He yelled it dozens of times. He called me names, with lots of swearing. He jabbed the machete toward me over and over, taunting me to fire at him. I kept my aim toward him and tried to settle him down. He just kept going. He wouldn't let up. I was waiting for him to charge me. I had decided I had to shoot him if he came closer. But he didn't come any closer. We were both just locked there. It seemed like forever. I was scared to death. I tried to stay calm and tried to settle him down. But it didn't work. He just kept screaming and swinging the machete."

"What happened to the other officers?"

"Well, a short time later, five minutes, ten, I wasn't sure, it just seemed to take forever, but they finally showed up and parked on the street behind my police car. They came to my side, and I recall feeling like we now had control and that we could arrest this guy. But Burt wouldn't drop the machete, and as long as he held it, there was nothing we could do. But then he started walking slowly backwards. I figured he was going to try and get back into the house. That's when I remembered the girl. I had forgotten that there was, supposedly, a girl inside. I recalled from training and experience that we could not let him go inside. If he got inside, I knew we would have lost control. At several points, Your Honour, I was actually going to shoot him. But then, when he was about to open the door, one of the other officers charged him and knocked him forward into the porch. I jumped in, also, and we managed to pull him outside."

"Then what happened?" the Crown asked.

As the lawyer asked this, I felt my heart begin to race. I knew that, shortly, the facts of the beating would arise. I just knew that the defence lawyer would be all over me, and I could almost feel him adjust his position in his seat as he got ready to pounce on me, but I remained calm and explained. "Well, Your Honour, all three of us tried pinning him to the ground to get the handcuffs on. But he was like a man possessed. I couldn't believe how strong he was, and he actually started to stand while we were still hanging on to him."

As difficult as it was, I remained calm and continued. My heart was racing as I spoke.

"I started smashing him with my fists, Your Honour, in the ribs. It didn't seem to stop him. He actually didn't stop until I hit him with the pepper spray. That's when we were able to handcuff him."

The Crown asked, "What to you mean you 'hit' him with the pepper spray? Could you clarify that, please?"

"Well, I didn't mean I physically hit him. I meant I depressed the button to activate the spray. I then directed the spray into his eyes."

At any time, the judge can interrupt to clarify a point or ask a detail. The judge slowly removed his glasses and did something I had never seen a judge do before.

He looked at me.

I thought I was going to get sick right then and there.

The judge spoke. "You said you punched him. How many times did you punch him, Constable?"

I replied, "Many times, Your Honour, more than twenty, at least." I didn't look at the defence lawyer, but I imagined he had a smirk on his face.

As the judge looked at me, I took a breath. I wanted this to end. I just wanted to go home. Then the judge spoke a second time. "How hard did you punch him, Constable?"

I thought I was done. I had said I had punched him a lot, and now he was asking how hard. I couldn't believe this. I figured my career was about to take an ugly turn. I replied to the judge, "Your Honour, I whacked him as hard as I could, over and over. I smacked him in the ribs and back. Yes, I punched him good."

I had sealed my fate. The defence lawyer's smirk was now a broad smile. It was what he wanted to hear. He had waited for that moment to attack me on the stand. I was thinking that now the worst would happen, just as I had predicted.

Telling the court that I had "whacked" Burt was what the defence wanted to hear, but to my surprise, it was also what the judge wanted to hear. The judge understood what Burt had put me through, and he understood well that Burt was lucky to be alive. Still looking at me, the judge smiled.

"Excellent job, Constable. Excellent!" He then leaned back in his chair.

Realizing that the judge had sided with the actions I had taken, the defence lawyer slumped back in his chair and threw his arms upward in disgust. No matter what other evidence was presented, the judge, in his infinite wisdom, had already rendered his decision. It was clear to him that I had shown restraint. He knew that Burt was lucky to be alive, bruises and all. An exhilarating rush went through me. I knew that everything would be okay.

The defence declined to cross-examine me. The direction the judge had taken was clear, and it was obvious to the defence that the judge had sided with my actions. The defence had no other issue to pursue. He knew his client, Burt, was guilty. He stood and asked, "Your Honour, can we take a short recess?"

The judge replied, "Will you have any questions for this constable?"

"No, Your Honour."

The judge then stated, "You are free to go, Constable. Court will recess for fifteen minutes."

A short time later, the court proceeding reconvened, and the defence returned to the courtroom and entered a guilty plea on behalf of his client. Once the proceeding was complete, Burt was remanded in custody to await his pre-sentencing report.

I was done on the stand. I would not be charged or investigated. I was free to go. I could go home. I smiled inside and thought, *The rum will taste good tonight!*

— Chapter 21 —

A New Day

There is a test to help you decide whether or not your mission in life is complete. The test is simple. If you are alive, your mission is not complete.

The float back down to reality happened incredibly fast. Once the judge had made his decision, it was like tons of stress had been lifted from deep inside me. I didn't even follow the rest of Burt's proceedings. I did hear sometime later that he was sentenced to seven months in jail for his little escapade. I didn't really care what he got. I was just glad that Burt hadn't been killed, nor I or anyone else. There was no coroner's inquest, and that was just fine. I was not investigated or arrested. It was all good.

I slept well the night after the trial. It was a bonus that the next day was a well-earned day off. This new day brought a new lease on life. A whole new attitude and energy that I had not felt since before this whole standoff began. I was myself again.

After I awoke, showered, and dressed, I whipped up my favourite breakfast for my family and me. It consisted of homemade hash browns fried to a golden crisp, bacon sizzled to a light crunch, eggs over easy, and white toast with raspberry jam. Okay, I know whole wheat toast is healthier for you, but white just tastes better. My motto is "Eat what you enjoy, because you never know when your next meal might be."

It was a beautiful day. The forecast called for sun and warm temperatures. Following breakfast, I decided that a hike was in order. Some much-needed time with my family was going to be the theme of the day. We built some tuna sandwiches (with white bread), gathered drinks, and threw the camera into a pack. My family and I were set to go.

Then the phone rang. Diane answered, then looked at me. "It's for you. It's your office."

I took the phone and said, "Hello." It was Dispatch.

"Oh, hi, Frank. I'm really sorry to bother you on your day off."

"No problem. What's up?"

"Well, Tony called in sick this morning, so Gina is on shift by herself. We just got a call about a domestic dispute. She needs backup. Can you come to work?"

— Epilogue —

When I graduated from Depot in October 1981, each of my troop mates and I purchased a small token to celebrate our time together. It was a gold miniature of our police badge, about the size of a dime. Each one was unique and individual. Although they were identical in form, the bottom was laser printed with our individual regimental numbers. Nobody else in the whole Royal Canadian Mounted Police organization had, or will ever have, that number. It is unique to each member. The miniature badge had a small hole at the top, which allowed a thin gold chain to be threaded, so it could be worn on one's neck like a military dog tag. I wore mine proudly. I never took it off. It was my connection to what I had been through to get where I was back then. I cherished it.

One day, when my son was about four years old, he noticed it around my neck and asked if he could wear it. Young boys and girls do that. They are inquisitive and want to learn and be a part of things. I completely understood his desire to try it out!

I took it off my neck and put it around his. He looked excited and proud. Off he ran, playing with his sister, running around the house, having fun, doing what kids do, and maybe even having a game of hopscotch.

A couple of hours later, my wife and I put together a nice dinner, and we called the children. My son showed up—minus the neck chain!

I stayed calm and asked, "Where is the neck chain?"

His response was nothing but a blank look. He was just a child. He had no idea where it was. At four years old, he had probably already forgotten he had been wearing it. I was devastated. He had lost the chain that I had been wearing for eight years.

He had no explanation, which was understandable. Hours of searching turned up nothing. It was gone. I was angry, but I didn't let him know. He was just a child. My badge and necklace were gone, but life would go on.

That was in 1989.

I thought about that chain for years, wondering where it had gone. With my new warped habit of thinking, I even wondered if some other kid had stolen it from around my son's neck. Regardless, it was gone. I may have reminded him over the years how he had lost the necklace—just to rub it in.

But there is an old saying: What goes around comes around. In the year 2002, I was stationed in a small town in Newfoundland. This would have been 7,000 kilometres from where my miniature badge had disappeared. While in this small town, I picked up the mail one day, just before Christmas, and there was a Christmas card from a couple I had not heard from in thirteen years. The couple were my former landlords, the owners of the home I had rented at the time my miniature badge had disappeared. Once I got home, I opened the card. All I could say was, "You have got to be kidding me!"

Inside the card was my miniature police badge with the necklace attached, as shiny and intact as the day it had disappeared.

In a note attached to the card, my former landlords explained that they had done a major renovation to the house I had rented so many years ago and found the badge inside a baseboard heater. They then made inquiries through their local police office to track me down and send me the badge. Just in time for Christmas!

I was thrilled to have it back, but I felt there was only one thing to do. I repackaged it, then mailed it to my son. He received it a few days after Christmas. I had also written a note with the necklace explaining its journey. He was even more thrilled than I to receive it. He told me that he had cried. He never lost it again!

My thirty-two years as a Mountie now seem like a brief flash in time. That's ironic, considering the many events throughout those years that had seemed to last a lifetime. Pretty much every day there are reminders that cause me to flash back to my years in the organization. Some of the reminders come from movies and television, even though most of what's on the small screen is laughable. Rarely a day will pass where there is not some story in the news relevant to the actions of the police. The media is always on top of them. I guess this is okay. It just adds a degree of accountability and keeps the police in line.

Even though many of the complaints I attended over the years involved carnage and inexplicable human travesties, I feel fortunate to have been there. Much of what I have witnessed has given me a greater understanding and appreciation of what life really is, and having escaped most of these events relatively unscathed is a bonus.

Still, today, if I see a police car drive by, I can't help but wonder aloud, "What's going on? Where is he or she going?" I feel left out. I feel the phone should ring from Dispatch, asking for my assistance. I just know I could help.

My back still hurts every day, and it always will, but that's okay. Feeling that pain is a reminder that I am still alive. I know things could have been much worse. That injury doesn't prevent me from doing most of what I love to do—outdoor things, mostly—and of course I have my workshop. I spend hours at the craft of woodworking. I may even build another little red Cross one day, but I doubt it would be as durable and long-lasting as my first.

In December of 2007, just when I thought my career was long past, I had the honour of attending Depot one more time. With incredible pride, at an RCMP graduation ceremony, I presented a police badge to my very own daughter, Kyra-Lee. Well, technically she is a stepdaughter, but she means more to me than that title reflects. That in itself seemed like yesterday and now nine years have passed.

Then, just when I thought there was nothing more to experience in this great life, my son, Ryan, comes along and presents me with a beautiful granddaughter, Olivia. And not to be outdone, my stepson, Travis, presents twin granddaughters, Aimsley and Emery. The great surprises just never end.

I never saw Burt again following that standoff. I closed that chapter and moved on. I just pray that he has found peace with whatever issues motivated him to act as he had. Walking out of court that day and not looking back was easy. I was always like that. I found it easy to move on.

Even though I miss it today, I was ready to leave police work. The time was right. I didn't really retire—I just moved on. Every week now I am doing something different. The change has been good. There were lots of positives about moving on, but probably the best part of retiring from police work was the fact that I could quit eating bullets. I never did like them, anyway!

THE END

Now I am ten-thirty-five.
Police lingo for "off duty."

— Acknowledgements —

One evening several months ago, I was enjoying a lovely dinner with Lloyd and Sandy Hollett of Pasadena, Newfoundland, friends of almost forty years. Following that meal, while sipping on a glass of wine, I told several stories about the things I had witnessed during my time with the Royal Canadian Mounted Police. My listeners responded with, "Oh my God, that's amazing. You should write a book!" I dismissed those comments as coming from friends who were just being polite. However, they persisted with their support and encouragement. Lloyd, the author of *Butterfly Messengers*, eventually convinced me that a book was in order, so I began typing. I doubt these stories would have ever come to print without the encouragement of the Holletts, and for that I thank them.

As with most compositions, this book required some editing once the initial draft was complete. I enlisted the expertise of Guy Romaine, a retired schoolteacher also residing in Pasadena.

Guy's knowledge of grammar and English composition proved valuable in the completion of this project. His dedication and time is greatly appreciated.

The stories you have read are either true events, written exactly as they occurred, or they are adapted from true events. Those based on true events have been selectively altered: names have been changed, locations have not been specified, and exact details have been modified. This was done in an effort to protect the identities of those involved.

Francis Paul Pitts was born on August 19, 1958, in the community of Freshwater, Bell Island, Newfoundland and Labrador. He was the middle child in a close family of eleven children. Frank was very young when his father died, and his mother raised all eleven children on her own. Following graduation from St. Boniface High School in Wabana, Bell Island, Frank attended the College of Trades and Technology in St. John's and acquired a certificate of technology in forest resources, which aided him in landing employment with the Newfoundland Forest Service and later with Environment Canada.

While working one day, Frank had a chance encounter that motivated him to join the Royal Canadian Mounted Police. He decided to pursue a career with the RCMP in early 1980 and joined the organization in April 1981. He spent the next thirty-two years at twelve different posting assignments in the provinces of Newfoundland and Labrador, Prince Edward Island, and British Columbia. In February 2009, he stayed for a brief assignment in Ottawa, Ontario, performing security duties during United States President Barrack Obama's visit to the Canadian capital city.

Frank's career earned him the Long Service Medals for twenty, twenty-five, and thirty years. In 1995, he was awarded a Commanding Officer's Commendation for outstanding and dedicated service during his assistance in resolving the infamous Gustaffson Lake Standoff in 100 Mile House, British Columbia, which ended without loss of life. In March 2010, Frank was awarded a Certificate of Appreciation, and a further Commanding Officer's Certificate of Appreciation, in recognition for his dedicated service and exemplary performance of duties as a member of the integrated security unit for the Vancouver 2010 Olympic and Paralympic Winter Games.

Frank Pitts retired in 2014 and moved to Pasadena, Newfoundland and Labrador, where he resides with his wife, Diane. In his spare time, he works on construction and maintenance projects in his woodworking shop.